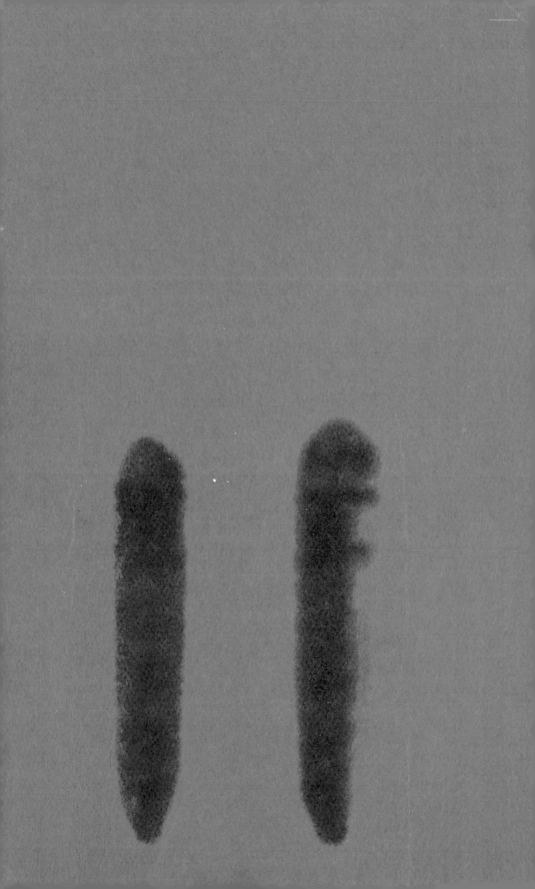

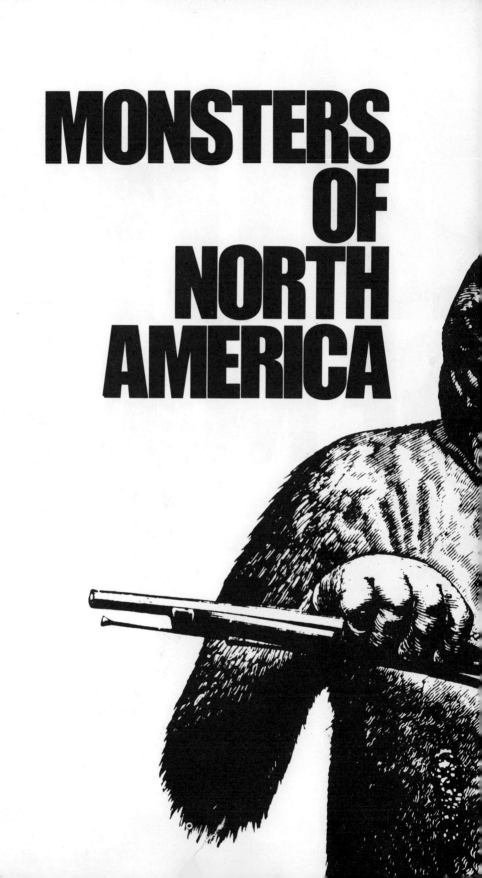

MONSTERS OF NORTH AMERICA

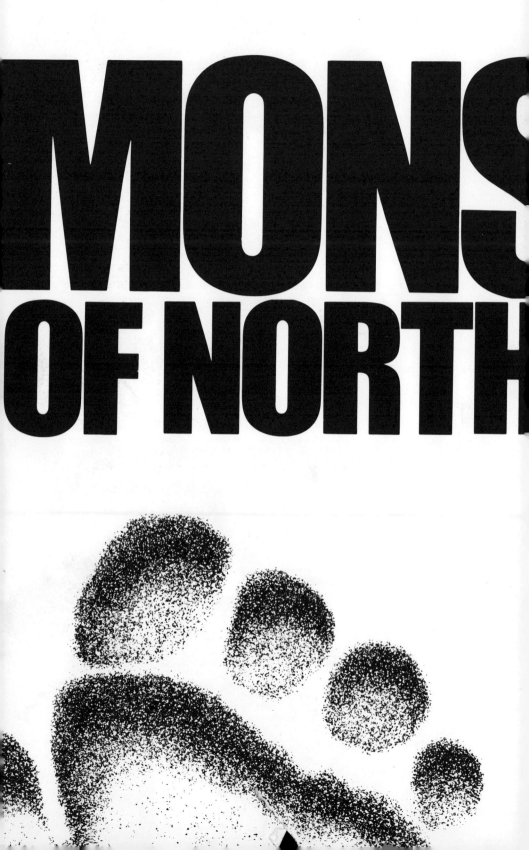

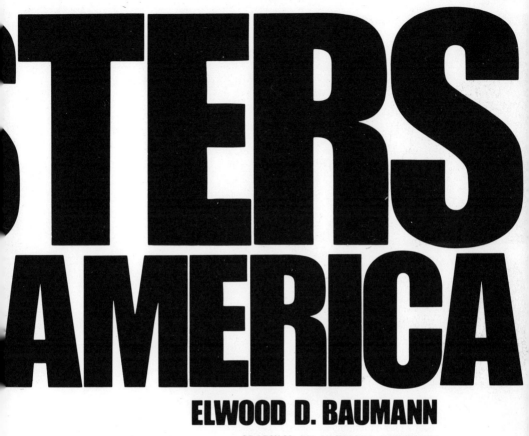

STERS
AMERICA

ELWOOD D. BAUMANN

GRAPHICS BY NICHOLAS KRENITSKY

Franklin Watts
New York/London/1978

Library of Congress Cataloging in Publication Data

Baumann, Elwood D.
  Monsters of North America.

  Bibliography: p.
  Includes index.
  SUMMARY: Presents accounts of encounters
with six unidentified creatures in the United States
and Canada.
  1. Monsters—Juvenile literature. [1. Monsters]
I. Title.
QL89.B4   001.9′44′0973   78-3703
ISBN 0-531-02246-3

CONTENTS

MONSTERS OF NORTH AMERICA

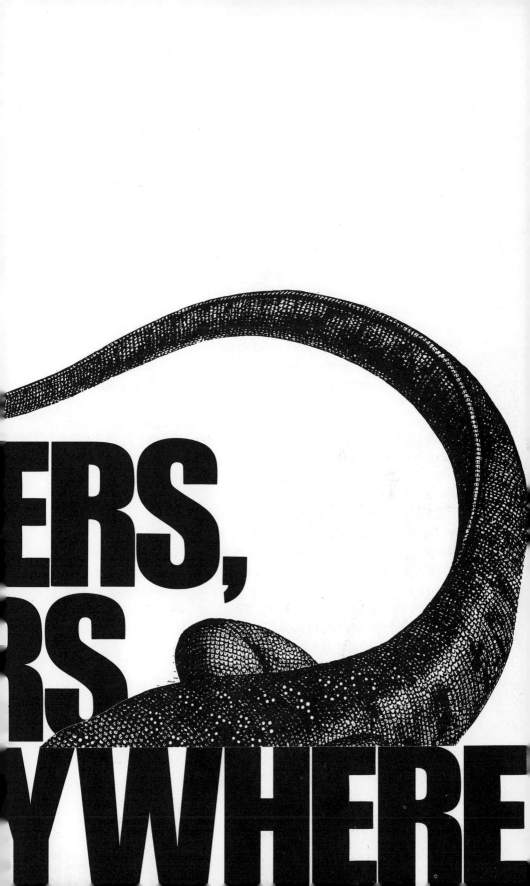

There is something about monsters that has always fascinated people. Fire-breathing dragons, man-eating giants, and huge winged serpents figured strongly in many ancient legends. Greek mythology described nine-headed water serpents, flying horses, a beast that was half lion and half eagle, hairy giants who had one eye in the middle of their foreheads, and a host of other weird creatures. Cave paintings of giants and strange beasts have been discovered in many parts of the world.

Man's fascination with monsters is just as great today as it was in ages past. Newspapers excitedly report every sighting. Monsters always make big news, and crowds of curious people invariably rush to the place where the creature was seen. Many of them are carrying cameras, but getting a photograph of a monster requires an awful lot of luck.

It's not surprising, of course, that Hollywood cashed in on our fascination with monsters. Hideous creatures of every description appeared on the screen. Some were ridiculous in the extreme, but one giant captured the imagination of everyone who saw him. The name of that giant was King Kong.

King Kong was an enormously successful movie. It made piles and piles of money, and it deserved to. The huge gorilla who starred in the film appeared so real that it was easy to forget that it was a man-made monster. People sat on the edge of the seat in rapt attention as the great hairy giant went on the rampage through the streets of New York. The film ended with the death of King Kong, and there was always a sigh of sadness from the audience. Although the monster had terrorized a city, nobody really wanted it to be killed.

None of the monsters that have been sighted in the United States and Canada is anywhere near as large as King Kong, of course. They may be only minimonsters by comparison, but they're still pretty big fellows indeed. Plaster of Paris casts have been made of footprints twenty-two inches (55.88 cm) long, and feet that size could belong only to a very large creature.

Getting an accurate description of a monster is a terribly difficult task. In the great majority of cases, the creature is seen for
only a very few seconds at the most. The sighting may occur in a
dense forest or a dark swamp. More frequently, it is seen hurry-
ing across a road at night. The driver suddenly sees something
strange in the glare of his headlights, then the something dis-
appears into the fields or forest. The man behind the wheel knows
that he's seen something out of the ordinary, but there's simply
no way in which he could describe it in any detail.

Police and reporters know that most people have great difficulty in describing a situation accurately. Ten witnesses, for example, may see a robber running from a bank, and the police may
be given five or more different descriptions. They might be told
that the bank robber was tall and short, fat and thin, young and
old, and had light and dark hair. Descriptions of monsters vary
even more dramatically because people are then trying to describe something which is totally unfamiliar to them.

Eyewitness reports are seldom completely reliable, and we can
easily understand why. A man driving a car just doesn't have the
time to study the creature he's seen. Neither does the man who
sights one in a swamp or forest. Both man and monster will try
to get out of there just as quickly as possible, and we can't blame
them for that. We're all afraid of the unknown, and a man who
comes face-to-face with a monster is not going to hang around
hoping to get a closer look. He may be curious, yes, but his safety
is going to be his first concern.

Up to now nobody has managed to get even a reasonably decent photograph of any of North America's unidentified monsters.
There have, however, been two close misses. Cloyce Warren
snapped a quick photo of the White River Monster in the act of
submerging, and Sallie Ann Clarke took a flash photo of the Lake
Worth Monster crashing through the brush. Unfortunately, both
photos were blurred and lacked detail. Scientists who studied
them were unable to reach any conclusions at all.

The monsters of North America have actually become a bit of an embarrassment to the scientific world. They want one of the creatures to be killed or captured so that they can study it in their laboratories. The lack of photographic evidence and the confusing reports of eyewitnesses worry them. Very few men of science seriously doubt the fact that huge unidentified creatures still roam the North American continent, but they want to see one with their own eyes. They demand proof, and about the only proof they will accept is a monster itself—dead or alive.

If it weren't for the great number of unexplained tracks found in so many parts of Canada and the United States, certain scientists would probably be tempted to put monsters out of their minds for once and always. The fact is, though, that these tracks do exist. And they're not hoaxes, either. They were made by large creatures still unknown to science. To complicate matters even more, one set of tracks may be very different from another. Footprints made by both three-toed and five-toed animals have been discovered in various places.

Although the tracks are interesting, they don't tell us very much about the creatures who made them. It's impossible to tell what they look like, but at least it's possible to get a rough idea of the size of the monster. Zoologist Ivan Sanderson, who studied a set of tracks on a Florida beach, said, "Whatever made these prints must have been about ten feet [3 m] tall and probably weighed about one thousand pounds [454 kg]." Then he added, "I'd give my right arm to get a good close look at the darn thing."

John Green, Canada's foremost authority on unidentified animals, is firmly convinced that there are a lot more monsters on the North American continent than people would believe. There have been sightings from the Atlantic to the Pacific, and from the Gulf of Mexico to the Canadian Arctic. Practically every

Indian tribe had legends about strange creatures which had been seen from time to time. As early as 1831 the New York *Evening Post* reported that a huge bearlike monster had been seen chasing cattle on a Missouri ranch. The creature ran on its hind legs, however, so it could not possibly have been a member of the bear family. Monster reports have come in from Missouri fairly regularly since 1831, but none of the creatures has yet been identified.

Another interesting point is made by John Green. He believes that many sightings are never reported. People fear ridicule, and they're afraid that they'll be laughed at if they say that they've seen a monster. There are numerous cases, too, where sightings have been reported to the police or press, but the witnesses asked that their names not be used. Some witnesses said nothing about what they had seen until other people had reported their own experiences.

Those who say that monsters couldn't possibly survive in a country as densely populated as the United States really don't have a leg to stand on. There are still vast areas of wilderness left in our country. Monsters most likely hide out during the day and do their traveling at night. This wouldn't present much of a problem to a creature of the wild. Even a very large animal can hide itself very effectively in a relatively small patch of brush.

Only on very rare occasions have monsters been seen during the daylight hours. The overwhelming majority of sightings have taken place at night, and a few have occurred at dawn or dusk. Ron Stewart, a California monster hunter, believes that the creatures could easily travel considerable distances during the hours of darkness. Their travels, of course, would sometimes take them across open country, and it's at such times that they might be seen by passing motorists.

Monsters occasionally pop up in the most unlikely places. The lead article in the September 1977 issue of *Fate* magazine is entitled "Monsters on the Loose." It was written by Dr. Louis Wiedemann. Several large unidentified creatures have been seen in New Jersey in recent years, and the article describes the reactions of people who claim to have seen them. It does not, however, make any attempt to identify the creatures.

New Jersey! Now that's just about the last place that anyone would expect to find a monster. New Jersey is one of our most densely populated states. It's very close to New York City and tens of thousands of people travel to the city every day to work. There are still fairly large tracts of forest in New Jersey, it's true, but it seems strange that these creatures would willingly come so close to the heavily populated areas.

The same thing has happened in other parts of the United States and Canada. Monster reports have come in from areas lying very close to Baltimore, Maryland; New Orleans, Louisiana; Fort Worth, Texas; and Vancouver, British Columbia. These are all large cities, and we would hardly think of them as monster country.

Ron Stewart has his own theory, and a number of scientists tend to agree with him. The monsters, he feels, are only temporary visitors to the heavily populated areas. They're shy creatures by nature and ordinarily try to stay as far away from man as possible. Once in a great while, though, their curiosity gets the better of them, and it's at such times that they wander off to have a good look around. After their curiosity has been satisfied, they again return home to their dense forest or dark swamp.

This theory seems to make sense. Quite a large number of farmers have reported strange tracks on their property. In several cases the creatures appear to have made a complete tour of inspection. Tracks led all the way around the house, barn, and other buildings. One farmer even had his tractor visited on three consecutive nights. When he decided to have a look at the monster, however, he ran into a problem: his dog stubbornly refused to follow the tracks into the swamp, and the farmer was reluctant to go in alone.

Because of its great size and strength, a monster could almost certainly tear a person into shreds. This has never happened, though. The monsters seem to be shy and perhaps even gentle creatures. The Fouke Monster is the only one that has ever been accused of attacking a human being, and that attack may not have been deliberate. It seems quite possible that the monster was as frightened as Bobby Ford himself. In its mad rush to get back to the safety of the swamp, it probably pushed Bobby roughly aside and inflicted a few scratches and bruises. At any rate, Bobby was not badly hurt. He was scared half to death, of course, but his physical injuries actually amounted to very little. Bobby was hospitalized because he had been frightened into a state of shock, not because he had sustained any serious injuries.

The monsters of North America may be huge and powerful, but we have no reason at all to think that any of them would attack without provocation. Although it's true that they've frightened some people badly, they can hardly be blamed for that. After all, it's not their fault if they meet someone while searching for food or having an innocent look around a farmyard.

Arkansas, Washington, California, and several other states have passed laws granting full protection to their monsters. This is encouraging news. They don't know how many monsters there are, and they want to protect those that they do have. The laws, however, do not apply to scientific expeditions or to those who are trying to bring one back alive.

Let the scientists have a few for their laboratories by all means.

But let the rest of the monsters go peacefully about their own business as they have done for so many hundreds of years.

Fouke is a sleepy little town in Arkansas. Only about three hundred people live there. The place has a café, a gas station, and a couple of stores, and that's about all. Hardly anyone had ever even heard of Fouke until the monster came to town. Since that happened, nothing in Fouke has been quite the same.

There had been several reports of monsters in the Fouke area over the years, but this was the first one to make a nuisance of itself. It happened late on the night of May 1, 1971.

Mrs. Jean Ford was lying on a couch in the living room when she noticed a curtain moving and saw a hand coming through the window beside her. "Only it wasn't really a hand," she reported later. "At first I thought it was a bear's paw, but it didn't look like that. It had heavy hair all over it and it had claws."

"I could see its eyes," Mrs. Ford went on. "They looked like coals of fire . . . real red. It didn't make any noise—except you could hear it breathing."

Jean Ford's screams brought her husband racing into the living room. He got there just in time to see a large creature of some sort moving away from the window. It was black and hairy and appeared to be at least six feet (1.8 m) tall. There was a rifle behind the kitchen door and Bobby Ford grabbed it with both hands.

The nearly full moon cast ghostly shadows on the lawn. All was quiet, but Bobby held his rifle at the ready. His heart was hammering because he didn't know what sort of creature he was up against. Although the thing hadn't harmed his wife, it had given her a terrible fright.

Just a few seconds after coming outdoors, Bobby got the worst scare of his life. Something leaped at him from the shadows, and he felt a stinging pain in his arm and side. The rifle was knocked out of his hands, and Bobby bolted for the house. He was running so fast that he ran straight through the unopened screen door. "I've never seen anyone so scared," said Jean Ford. "He was completely out of his head. Raving like a madman."

It was a dreadful time for Mrs. Ford. The car was outside, and so was the monster. She knew, though, that she couldn't stay in the house any longer. The monster could come crashing in at any moment. Besides, her husband needed help. Summoning up all her courage, she hurried Bobby out to the car and drove over to the home of the local policeman.

Constable Ernest Walraven realized at once that the Fords had had some sort of frightening experience. Jean Ford was shaking like a leaf. Bobby was in even worse condition. He kept raving on and on about being attacked by a monster. Walraven had no idea what he was talking about, but he knew that something had to be done for him. Although it was well after midnight, the constable drove the couple to a hospital in Texarkana. Bobby was treated for shock, and the scratches on his arm and side were looked after.

The Fords spent the rest of the night with Constable Walraven. There was a monster around their house, and they were too frightened to return before daylight. When the sun came up, they would go back to the house and pack their things. They had rented the house from Martin Crank only five days earlier, but both of them agreed that they would never be able to spend another night in the place. It would mean living in constant fear, and they weren't prepared to do that. They would have to move immediately.

The three people arrived at the old Crank home at dawn. Bobby Ford showed the constable where he had been attacked, and Walraven had a look around. He knew, though, that the chances of finding anything were pretty remote. It had rained the night before, so it would be difficult to follow any tracks he might find.

At any rate, the tracks would soon be lost. Boggy Creek flowed into the Sulphur River Bottoms just a short distance from the house. This was an enormous swamp area large enough to hide any number of monsters.

Another element was added to the mystery while Walraven was still making his tour of investigation. A neighbor stopped by and told him that he had heard a strange howling noise during the night. "It came from the woods or the swamp. I couldn't tell which," he said. "It sounded just like a woman screaming at the top of her voice, but I know it was some kind of animal."

But what kind of an animal? wondered Walraven. Did monsters scream? He didn't know. He only knew that Bobby Ford had said that he had been attacked by a monster and that the neighbor had heard some strange creature screaming at night.

It was all very confusing, but there was more to come.

By the middle of the morning, everyone in Fouke had heard about the monster. Several of those who believed the story had a theory of their own. "It's probably the same monster that scared those folks over in Jonesville a few years back," suggested one.

"If it's the same one my sister saw, it's getting on in years," said another. "She saw it when she was ten and she's seventy-eight now."

"I'll bet a dollar it was a panther," declared an old-timer. "There's always been panthers in the swamps, and they scream just like a woman."

"Jackie Olden says he saw a monster in his pasture about twenty or twenty-five years ago," another volunteered. "He emptied his rifle at it, but he was shaking so much that he couldn't have hit the side of a barn."

Monsters always make big news, and the Fouke Monster was no exception. The story first appeared in the Arkansas papers and was then grabbed up by the wire services. Many millions of people throughout the world learned that a man in Arkansas had been attacked by a monster. It was the sort of thing they loved to read about, and everyone was eager to hear more.

Sleepy little Fouke suddenly found itself on the map, and the monster was its most famous citizen.

PHENOMENON

For some strange reason the editor of one of the Arkansas news-papers took a great dislike to the word *monster*. One of the dic-tionary definitions of *monster* is "a fabulous or actually existing animal of strange, grotesque, or horrible form." This would cer-tainly apply to the creature seen around Fouke, but the editor used the title the Fouke Monster only on very rare occasions.

This particular editor almost always referred to the creature as the Fouke Phenomenon. According to Webster's *New Col-legiate Dictionary,* second edition, a phenomenon is "an excep-tional or abnormal person, thing, or occurrence." The Fouke Monster—or the Fouke Phenomenon—also fits this definition, so we can hardly say that the editor was wrong. To the rest of the world, however, the creature was known only as the Fouke Monster.

To the amusement of some and the annoyance of others, the little Arkansas community suddenly discovered that it was an important tourist center. Three men who were not at all amused were Miller County Sheriff Leslie Greer, Constable Ernest Wal-raven, and Mayor John Larey. "We've got a whole pack of armed idiots over here hunting the monster, and somebody's going to get hurt," moaned Sheriff Greer.

The sheriff had good reason to be worried. Men carrying every-thing from knives to automatic rifles were prowling through the woods and the Sulphur River Bottoms. The woods were dan-gerous enough, but the swamp was much worse. Anyone un-familiar with the area could get hopelessly lost in the trackless quagmire. It would then be the sheriff's job to go into the swamps and try to find the lost monster hunter.

Constable Ernest Walraven had his problems as well. Several weeks after the Bobby Ford incident, three men from Texarkana identified as Lou Harvin, Floyd Thomas, and Bob Williams came charging into his office. "We've been attacked by the monster!" they cried out.

Walraven was too good a policeman to be taken in so easily.

The men were covered with scratches, but none of them was serious. Neither were they trembling in terror as the Fords had been. The constable suspected a hoax, and his suspicions were confirmed. He examined material beneath the men's nails and charged them with having scratched one another. State Trooper Marvin Sinyard agreed, and the three men were ordered to post a bond of sixty dollars each for disturbing the peace.

None of the three men has been seen in Fouke since.

Reports of sightings kept coming in. Mr. and Mrs. D. C. Woods and Mrs. R. H. Sedgass almost ran into it on Highway 71 late one night. "It had long, dark hair and it ran upright like a man, but much faster," reported Mrs. Sedgass. "Its arms were swinging kind of like a monkey's. The face was kind of like a monkey's, too, and I'd guess that it weighed way over two hundred [90 kg] pounds."

"I'm not laughing about this monster business now," said Mrs. Woods, "because I've seen the thing, and I know it's real."

A. L. Tipson and Robert Utke also saw the monster the same night. "Looked like one of those things from that *Planet of the Apes* movie," said Utke, "except that this thing was a lot hairier."

"And a lot bigger," added Tipson.

Several Fouke residents reported having seen the monster, and quite a few more said that they had heard it screaming at night. Each report caused another little shudder of fear to ripple through the town. "The monster has been a source of mental anguish for the people of Fouke," reported radio station KAAY in Little Rock. "People in the Fouke area have been living on edge for weeks," declared the *Arkansas Democrat*. Miller County authorities realized that something had to be done, and an official monster hunt was organized.

Unfortunately, the hunt did little to calm the fears of the people of Fouke. In fact, it probably made them even more afraid. Dogs were unable to track the creature, but a most interesting and unusual footprint was found on the shore of Boggy Creek. It was fourteen inches long (35.6 cm) and five inches (12.7 cm) wide, and apparently had only three toes on each foot.

Frank Schambagh, an anthropologist at Southern State College in Magnolia, studied a plaster of Paris cast of the footprint and shook his head. "It's not human, and I'd rule out any type of monkey or ape," he declared. "All of them have five toes. Besides," he went on, "there have never been monkeys native to North America, so that eliminates anything that could have been left over from times past."

It wouldn't be quite right to say that everyone in Fouke was unhappy about the monster. Mr. and Mrs. Bill Williams at the Boggy Creek Café, for example, rather like the creature. Tourists crowd the café, and business has never been better. Besides the regular items on the menu, hungry diners can order a Three-Toed Sandwich, a Monster Delight, or a Monster Special.

A small souvenir shop has recently been added to the café. Curiosity seekers eagerly buy reproductions of the monster's footprint, key chains, postcards, and other items. By far the biggest sellers, of course, are ashtrays and bumper stickers which boldly proclaim Fouke—Home of the Fouke Monster.

Another man who is rather fond of the monster is Willie Smith, owner of the local gas station. Smith claims to have seen the creature on five separate occasions and says that it was somewhat smaller when he saw it for the first time in 1954. "Either it's grown up or it was a different monster I saw then," he says.

Many of the tourists who stop at Smith's gas station don't spend a penny. They're more interested in talking about the monster than they are in having their tanks filled. Fortunately, Willie Smith is a very friendly and easygoing Arkansan. "If folks want to stop by and ask me questions about the monster, that's all right with me," he insists, adding, "There's nothing else to do around this place anyway, and it's kind of nice to have someone to talk to."

Perry Parker, a Fouke schoolboy, is one of the monster's staunchest supporters. He has good reason to be. A car pulled up alongside him one afternoon, and the driver asked how he could find the house where the monster had attacked a man. Perry led the way over to the old Crank home and gave the driver and his passengers a guided tour. They were so grateful that they gave him two dollars.

From that moment on, Perry was in business. Whenever a car stopped in front of the Crank home, he was there to meet it. Visitors were shown the exact spot where the creature had leaped out at Bobby Ford and the screen door he had smashed through. They were also led down to Boggy Creek, and the huge swamp area was pointed out to them. The majority of people paid Perry for the tour, and he was soon the richest boy in town.

"As far as I'm concerned," he declared happily, "that monster is the best thing that ever happened to Fouke."

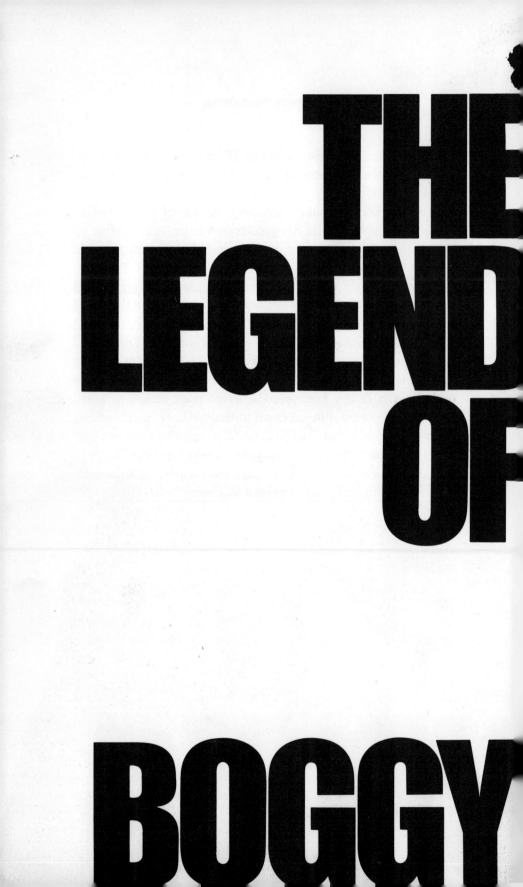

CREEK

Charles B. Pierce, a television producer and director from Texas, couldn't get his mind off the Fouke Monster. Thoughts of the creature plagued him day and night. It was constantly in the news, and he couldn't help wondering just what was going on in the little Arkansas community. Finally, he decided to drive over to Fouke and see for himself.

The visit made a deep and lasting impression on him. More than two hundred people claimed that they had seen a strange creature of some type. Others had heard it screaming at night. Pierce was forced to believe that most of the stories he heard were true. The residents of Fouke were honest and hardworking people who went to church every Sunday. They were not the kind of people to lie to a stranger.

When he had first read about the monster, Pierce had thought that it might make an interesting television program. After his visit to Fouke, however, he began planning on a much broader scale. He had been greatly moved by the sincerity of the people. They were living in fear of an unknown something, and Pierce wanted to tell their story to the world. The best way to do that, he decided, would be to produce a full-length movie.

The more Pierce thought about it, the more he liked the idea. Everyone was interested in monsters, and the Fouke Monster had been making headlines for months. If people enjoyed reading about monsters, then it was reasonable to suppose that they would also enjoy seeing a movie about one. It was a risk, yes, but it was a risk he felt he had to take.

Pierce decided from the very beginning that he would avoid any Hollywood-type sensationalism. "I'm not going to say whether or not there actually *is* a monster in the Sulphur River Bottoms," he told the Texarkana *Gazette*. "My film is going to be based on fact and fact alone. No hearsay will be used. I only want to tell the story as it actually happened. It will be up to the audience to make up their own minds."

Not a single Hollywood actor was to be used in the film. Pierce insisted upon reality, so the heroes and the heroines were the citizens of Fouke. There was not going to be any pomp or pageantry. Neither was there going to be any acting or dramatics. The people were simply going to be themselves. They would appear in the film as they appeared in their normal everyday lives.

The role of the monster was one of the toughest problems Pierce had to face. He knew he wouldn't have a King Kong-type creature, but that was about all he did know. Although many people had seen the thing, their descriptions varied drastically. Even the composite drawing made by Miller County Deputy Sheriff Roy Edwards didn't seem suitable. Edwards had taken down the descriptions of dozens of eyewitnesses, studied them carefully, then drew a large picture of what the monster supposedly looked like. Edwards himself cheerfully admitted that his drawing of the monster looked like nothing on earth—and he was right.

Nobody had ever come face to face with the Fouke Monster, so nobody was able to describe it accurately. This fact bothered Pierce for a long time. Then he had an idea! He would shoot his film so that people would catch only fleeting glances of the monster. They would also see its shadow, but there would be no close-ups. The actual appearance of the monster would be left entirely up to the imagination of the audience.

Pierce called his film *The Legend of Boggy Creek*. It played in theaters from coast to coast and was a stunning success everywhere. The audiences loved the simple realism of the movie. There was no trace of sensationalism. The producer made no attempt to influence anyone's thinking, but there was no need to do that. The true story was convincing enough.

The film was charming in its simplicity. Few people had realized that there was so much savagely beautiful wilderness in southwestern Arkansas. They were surprised, too, to see the abundance of bird and animal life in the swamps. The tarpaper shacks and backwater shanties must also have come as a surprise to many people.

No one could possibly have doubted the sincerity of the people who described their encounters with the monster. They weren't actors, and there was no drama. They were simply being themselves. It was their honesty that made the monster become startlingly alive to the viewers.

The twang in the southwestern Arkansas speech added to the reality. "What kinda thing can pick up two hunnerd pound [90 kg] hawgs and walk off with 'em?" asked a farmer in overalls. "I seen it twice, and I hope I don't never see it no more," said a man standing on the dilapidated porch of his shanty. A grizzled old-timer in a slouch hat had met the monster one day while hunting in the woods. "If I'd'a shot that thing," he drawled, "and it turned out to be a man, I'd'a had to live with that for the rest o' my life."

Boggy Creek was narrated by a young man who was only seven years old when he first heard the creature's chilling scream. "It scared me then, and it scares me now," he declared. Pierce himself heard the monster scream several times and was once lucky enough to get a tape recording of it. The scream he recorded was heard frequently throughout the film, and it raised a lot of goosepimples.

The majority of people who saw the film were convinced that *The Legend of Boggy Creek* was more than a legend. An unknown something was terrorizing a small Arkansas community. It might be a monster, or it might be something else. This was something the viewers had to decide for themselves. Most people, of course, believed that it actually was a monster, because they *wanted* to believe that it was a monster.

Tourists became a familiar sight in Fouke. People had seen the movie, now they wanted to see the place where it had all happened. Willie Smith spent many long, happy hours answering questions. The owners of the Boggy Creek Café were kept busy selling Monster Specials and Monster Delights. Perry Parker began to charge a dollar for his guided tours and could hardly handle all his business.

The happiest man of all, though, was Charles B. Pierce. The success of his movie about the Fouke Monster had made him a very rich man.

A GREAT BIG THING CALLED

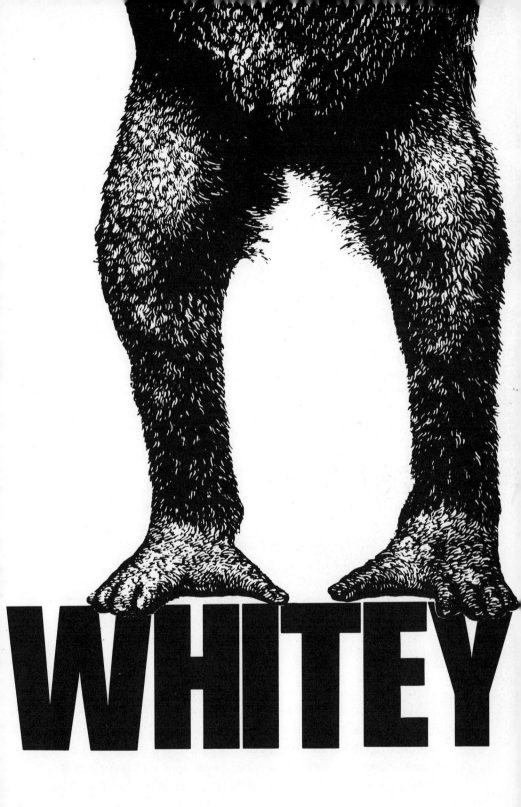

WHITEY

The Quapaw Indians told the early settlers in Newport, Arkansas about a very strange island in the White River. It would appear in different places from time to time, then not be seen again for a number of years.

One morning the island appeared just halfway across the river from the Indians' camp. The curiosity of a young brave was aroused, and he paddled out to have a closer look at it. It was not like any island he had ever seen before. The surface was white and slippery, and there was no vegetation at all. When the young brave poked at the island with his paddle, a small dent appeared in the side. This was indeed a peculiar situation. The island didn't really seem like an island at all. The Indian was more curious than ever, so he got out of his canoe and crawled on top of the island.

Then he got the surprise of his life! A part of the island seemed to be floating just beneath the surface of the water. But that wasn't all. One end of the island appeared to be shaped like a huge head. The other end rather resembled a tail.

The Indian decided that the smartest thing for him to do was to get back into his canoe and paddle out of there as fast as he could go. He didn't quite make it, however. The island suddenly began thrashing about violently. Spray flew in all directions, and the young brave was pitched off into the White River. While he raced for shore, the island raced swiftly downstream.

The early settlers smiled smugly when they were told about the island that had come to life. The Indians, they thought, were rather strange people, and they had some rather strange stories to tell.

The first references to an unidentified creature in the White River date back to about 1850. These stories, however, were shrouded in fable and myth. Few people lived in the Newport area at that time. Communications were poor and records were sketchy. The local farmers might tell one another that they had seen something strange in the river, but this fact would probably not have been entered in the archives.

People in the Ozarks love legends, and one of the strangest legends of all concerns their monster. It goes back to the time of the Civil War. A Confederate riverboat was steaming north with several million dollars in gold on board. It had just passed Newport when it received a violent blow in the bow. One blow followed another in rapid succession. The captain and crew watched in horror as a huge form kept crashing into their vessel. The stout planking was soon smashed to smithereens. A gaping hole appeared in the bow, and the riverboat and its cargo of gold sank to the bottom of the river.

No one takes that legend very seriously, of course, but it prompted one resident of Newport to tell me, "The only thing I have against that old monster is that it was on the wrong side during the Civil War."

The creature paid a brief visit to the Newport area in 1890, then sank completely out of sight. It was gone for so long that many people forgot that it had ever existed. Forty-seven years passed, in fact, before it returned to its old haunts in the White River.

It was in the summer of 1937 that the monster came swimming back. Early in July several of the town's most reputable citizens reported that they had seen something which they could neither explain nor understand. Two prominent businessmen reported seeing a tremendous disturbance in the river. Water flew in all directions and the waves rolled one hundred yards (91.4 m) upstream and down. Others reported seeing similar disturbances, and some claimed that they had seen a huge, light-colored form slicing through the water. They had no idea, though, what the creature could possibly be.

A man called Bramlett Bateman had a ringside seat for all the activity. His house was on the monster's favorite stretch of river, and he says that he saw it more than one hundred times in 1937 and 1938.

Bateman was not the most popular man in Newport. He charged people who came onto his land hoping to see the monster, and this didn't win him any friends. Some said that Bateman had never even seen the creature. He claimed so many sightings only because he wanted a lot of people to come onto his farm.

This accusation angered Bateman, and he stalked over to the courthouse on September 22, 1937. People didn't believe him, so he had decided to make a sworn statement and set the matter right. His affidavit read:

I, Bramlett Bateman, state under oath, that on or about the first of July, 1937, I was standing on the bank of White River about one o'clock and something appeared in the river, about 375 feet [113.75 m] from where I was standing, somewhere near the east bank of said river. I saw something appear on the surface of the water. From the best I could tell, from the distance, it would be about 12 feet long and 4 or 5 feet wide [3.66 m long, 1.21 or 1.51 m wide]. I did not see either head or tail, but it slowly rose to the surface and stayed in this position some five minutes. It did not move up or down the river at this particular time but afterward on many different occasions I have seen it move up and down the river, but I never have, at any time been able to determine the full length or size of said monster.

Some two weeks ago, from this date, September 22nd, 1937, I saw the same thing upstream about 200 yards [182 m] from where it made its first appearance. On the last day that I saw the monster it was in the current of the river. Before it was always seen in the eddy. There is no question in my mind whatever but that the monster remains in this stretch of river.

I can secure sworn affidavits from the following reputable citizens and landowners who have seen the same thing that I have: Z. B. Reid, Joe McCartney, Henry Harper, J. S. Defries and Norman Bundy. These I just happened to think of, but I can secure at least 25 other affidavits from people who have seen it.

Bateman's sworn statement appeared in the Newport *Daily Independent* and aroused tremendous interest. Everyone knew that a man wouldn't voluntarily make a sworn statement if he didn't mean every word he said. Besides, Z. B. Reid and Joe McCartney, two of the men he had mentioned, were Jackson County officials. The farmer would not dare to say that they had seen the monster unless they actually had seen it.

The people of Newport had given their monster the nickname "Whitey." They now knew that the Bateman farm was the best place to watch for Whitey, so hundreds of them paid Bramlett Bateman to tramp across his fields.

Then Whitey played a dirty trick on the Newport citizens. In the fall of 1938 it left the White River for parts unknown.

It was gone for thirty-three years.

In the middle of June 1971 Mike Masterson of the Newport *Daily Independent* received a most unusual phone call. "I don't want you to think I'm crazy," said an excited voice, "but I just saw a creature the size of a boxcar thrashing around in the White River."

"Who's speaking, please?" asked Masterson.

There was a brief pause, then, "I don't want you to use my name. I only want to tell you what I saw."

Masterson explained that he could not print the story if the man would not identify himself. He promised, however, not to reveal the caller's identity in the newspaper article. This satisfied the man, and he told the reporter who he was. Masterson gulped. The caller was one of Newport's most influential and respected citizens.

"I saw this thing from only about one hundred fifty feet [45.5 m] away." It was obvious to the reporter that the man was still extremely excited. "It had a smooth kind of skin, but it looked as though it was peeling off. Maybe they were scales. I don't know. I– I–"

"Yes, go on," said the reporter.

"Well, like I told you, it was the size of a boxcar," the voice continued. "I was on the shore and suddenly the water began to boil up about two or three feet [.60 or .91 m] high. Then this huge form comes rolling up. It just kept coming and coming until I thought it would never end."

The article appeared in the *Daily Independent* that evening, and Newport was delighted. Whitey had returned to its old haunts.

An old fisherman named Ernest Denks read the article about the monster and stopped in at the *Daily Independent*. Denks, it developed, had seen the monster the previous week. He had said nothing about it at the time, however, because he was afraid that people would laugh at him.

"This thing I saw must have weighed at least one thousand pounds [453.6 kg]," Denks told Orville Richolson, general manager of the newspaper. "It looked like something that came from the ocean. It was gray, real long, and had a long pointed bone protruding from its forehead. It was the darndest looking thing I've ever seen. When I saw it, I didn't hang around. I started the motor on my boat and got the heck out of there real fast."

"At what time of the day did you see this creature?" asked Richolson.

"It was in the evening," Denks replied, then quickly added, "I don't want anyone thinking I'm a drinker, Mr. Richolson. No, sir! I'm a God-fearing man and haven't touched liquor in thirty years."

After the reported sightings by the anonymous caller and Ernest Denks, things really began happening fast. On June 28, three Newport men spotted the monster while they were out fishing. It was no more than two hundred feet (60.66 m) from their boat. There was no warning, and the men were taken completely by surprise. They were concentrating on their fishing when the water between their boat and the shore suddenly began to churn. Then a giant form rose to the surface. Although the creature was visible for only a few seconds, one of the men managed to snap a fast photo.

Unfortunately, the photo did almost nothing to solve the mystery of the White River Monster. It was about as vague as the descriptions given by witnesses. It showed only a portion of what appeared to be a grayish creature sinking below the river's surface in a swirl of bubbles.

"My camera's only a cheap one, and I was shaking like a leaf when I took that picture," explained Cloyce Warren. "I don't mind telling you that I was scared to death. That thing looked like something prehistoric. It was over thirty feet [9.14 m] long. Its tail was thrashing constantly, and there were bubbles and foam all around the front of it." Then he said again, "I don't mind telling you that I was scared to death."

Lloyd Hamilton, the next man to get a photograph of Whitey, had even worse luck. He snapped a picture of a "great, big, huge spiny-backed monster" and was sure that his picture would be a good one. As luck would have it, though, he forgot to tell the photographer at the *Daily Independent* that he was using color film. The pictures were developed as black and white and showed absolutely nothing.

The excitement increased almost from day to day. Three weeks after Ernest Denks's sighting of the monster, two men stopped at the office of Jackson County Sheriff Ralph Henderson. They had beached their boat on Towhead Island, they reported, and both of them had seen some enormous tracks. Neither of them could even imagine what sort of a creature could leave tracks of such awesome dimensions.

Henderson and several other law enforcement officers took off within the hour. Towhead Island is located in a lonely stretch of river a few miles south of Newport. A sandy beach stretches the length of one side. Brush, high grass, and a few trees cover the rest of the island. The river flows slowly in this area and is over a hundred feet (30.33 m) deep.

The men found the tracks without difficulty and stood staring in amazement. They were gigantic! "What in the world do you suppose made those?" asked Game Warden Claude Foushee.

"It must have been Whitey," said State Trooper Ronnie Burke. "There's nothing else in Arkansas that could leave tracks that size."

"They could have been faked, you know," suggested Foushee.

"I don't think so." Sheriff Henderson shook his head, his eyes still focused on the tracks. "If someone faked these, he went to a heck of a lot of trouble and put them in a mighty unlikely place. Hardly anyone ever comes here." He paused for a moment, then said slowly, "No, I don't think they're faked."

The tracks were a whopping fourteen inches long and eight inches across (35.56 cm long, 20.33 cm across). There were three toes with claws, large pads on the heel and toes, and a spur sticking out at an angle from the heel. There was a distance of eight feet between each track. The sheriff estimated the tracks to be about three weeks old, which coincided with the time of Denks's sighting.

While the sheriff and two deputies made plaster of Paris casts of the tracks, Game Warden Foushee went exploring. At the upper end of the island, he came across another set of tracks. They led to a grassy area close to the shore. The grass had been smashed flat as if something big and heavy had been lying on it. Foushee had a quick look around, then hurried back to get the sheriff and his deputies.

"Boys," said Sheriff Henderson after studying the tracks and flattened grass, "we've got a mystery on our hands, and it looks to me like it's a mighty big one."

Whitey simply could not keep his name out of the newspapers during the summer of 1971. On July 23, a headline in the *Arkansas Gazette* declared "Something Large and Alive Lifted Boat, 2 Monster Hunters Report."

Ollie Ritcherson and Joey Dupree were not actually hunting the monster when they got themselves into trouble. They were trying to catch some catfish. The incident occurred between Bateman's Bend and Towhead Island. This was the stretch of river where Whitey had been sighted most frequently, and perhaps he didn't like the idea of anyone else catching fish which he thought belonged to him.

"I've fished that part of the river all my life and I know every inch of it," said Ritcherson. "There was no debris in sight, and you don't find tree stumps in water a hundred [30.33 m] feet deep. Our boat was lifted completely out of the water and turned halfway around," he went on. "Whatever it was that came up under us was very large and very much alive."

Dupree agreed. "It wasn't no stump or log," he declared. "We were just suddenly lifted up and turned sideways. We were both scared pretty bad, and we got the heck out of there as fast as we could."

Shortly after the Ritcherson and Dupree experience, the monster put on a free show for the Richard McClaughlin family of Lincoln, Nebraska. They were having a picnic lunch on the bank of the river, McClaughlin told Sheriff Henderson, when a giant form rose to the surface. It seemed to have a head of some kind and a spiny backbone. It was very long and light gray in color. "I'd estimate its length at between sixty and seventy-five feet [18.29 m and 22.75 m]," said McClaughlin, "and I couldn't even begin to estimate how much it must have weighed." The creature thrashed around on the surface for nearly five minutes before submerging.

"You must have seen Whitey," said Sheriff Henderson.

"Whitey?" McClaughlin looked puzzled. "Who's Whitey?"

"The White River Monster," Henderson explained.

"The White River Monster?" The puzzled look was still on McClaughlin's face. "I've never heard of it," he said. "We're from Nebraska, you know, and we've never been in Arkansas before."

Whitey may have been only a local curiosity in 1971, but it soon became internationally famous. Dr. Dillon Ripley of Washington's Smithsonian Institution came to Newport to see what he could learn. Scientists from other institutions followed. Unfortunately, they didn't learn very much. Whitey refused to show itself, and the descriptions given by witnesses were too vague to be of any real value.

The investigators didn't have any luck at all with Bramlett Bateman. "I saw the monster over a hundred times in 1937 and 1938, and that's all I'm saying," he told one scientist. "I told the truth then, and I'm telling the truth now."

"Have you seen it since it came back this summer?" the scientist asked.

"Sure," replied Bateman. "Lots of times."

"Can you tell me what it looked like?" the man of science inquired.

"Looked just like it looked when I saw it in '37 and '38," was Bateman's reply.

A television crew from Columbia Broadcasting System didn't fare much better. Bateman refused to be interviewed. He also refused to appear on a single foot of film. The cameramen weren't too terribly unhappy about this, though. They knew that there were plenty of other people in the Newport area who would be only too pleased to appear on television and tell what they had seen.

The Columbia Broadcasting System people had barely left town when a Japanese television crew arrived. They were going to film a documentary on the monster for Nippon Television. They had plenty of money to spend, and everyone except Bramlett Bateman cooperated with them. Cloyce Warren showed them his photograph of Whitey. Sheriff Henderson showed them his plaster of Paris casts and took them out to Towhead Island. Ollie Ritcherson and Joey Dupree pointed out the place where something large and alive had lifted their boat out of the water.

The cooperation delighted the television crew, and they were all smiles when they set out on their long trip back to Japan.

The publicity was good for business, so the Newport Chamber of Commerce decided to put on a publicity stunt of its own. Charles A. Brown, a diver, was hired to make an underwater search for the monster. The news agencies were given the story, and the citizens of Newport got ready for action.

And they got it! Newspapermen, movie cameramen, and tourists from all over Arkansas and neighboring states came piling into the little town on the White River. All had to pay a small fee to watch the proceedings from the search area. The Chamber of Commerce sold cold drinks and sandwiches. A platform for dancing had been erected on the river bank, and fiddlers happily ground out hillbilly tunes.

The noise and excitement may have been too much for Whitey. At any rate, poor Brown didn't see anything of interest. He dutifully spent an entire day paddling around in the murky waters, but it was a waste of time. The monster, he concluded, must have moved either upstream or downstream.

Whitey had become an important tourist attraction, and the state government decided that their famous visitor deserved protection. It was therefore resolved in the Senate of the Sixty-Ninth General Assembly of the state of Arkansas that

The part of the White River in Arkansas from a southern point at Old Grand Glaize, Arkansas, to a northern point near Rosie, Arkansas, is the natural habitat of the White River Monster, and that this part of the White River be set aside and known henceforth as "White River Monster Sanctuary and Reserve" and that it is unlawful to molest, kill, trample or harm the White River Monster while in its native habitat.

It's nice to know that it is unlawful to molest, kill, trample, or harm the White River Monster. It would also be nice to know just what sort of a creature Whitey actually is. Many people think that it originally came from the ocean. This is possible, of course. The White River flows into the Mississippi, which in turn flows into the Gulf of Mexico.

Descriptions are so vague and so varied that it's difficult to know just what to think. Some say that it might be a giant sturgeon. Or a giant gar. Or a giant catfish. The late zoologist and monster hunter Ivan T. Sanderson thought that a huge Mississippi alligator (Alligator *mississippienses*) may have caused some of the reports. Others suggest that it might be a dugong or a manatee. Still others readily admit that they don't have the foggiest idea what it is that has been splashing around in the White River from time to time for more than one hundred twenty-five years.

Common sense tells us that a monster like Whitey could not possibly exist. The facts are, though, that something left tracks on Towhead Island. Something showed up on Cloyce Warren's photograph. Something lifted Ollie Ritcherson's boat out of the water. Something which cannot be logically explained has been seen by dozens of level-headed Arkansans.

The mystery of the monster's identity may never be solved, but Bill Heard of the Chamber of Commerce isn't worried about that. "We don't know what kind of a creature Whitey is," he says, "and that's not really important. The important thing is that the monster decided to return to Newport, and all of us here were glad to see it back."

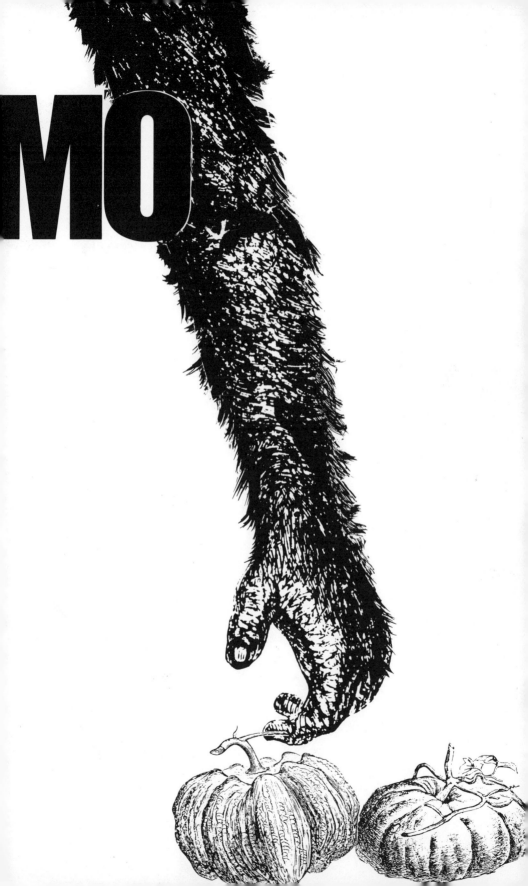

In the late summer of 1972 an unidentified creature that later became known as Momo created havoc in Pike County, Missouri. Dogs howled at night. Cattle and horses stampeded wildly in the pastures. Fruit disappeared from the trees. Pumpkins, squashes, and melons were pulled from the vines. Something was wrong, but it didn't occur to anyone that the nightly visitor might be a monster.

Johnnie Johnson and Pat Gorman were among the first ones to see it. They were fishing bullheads one night on the Cuivre River when they heard a soft splashing sound a short distance upstream. Johnson's Alsatian was with them, and the dog was wild with fear. It cowered at Johnson's feet, whining piteously. Its tail was between its legs, its hair stood straight up on end.

Johnson bent down to pat his dog, then snapped rigidly erect. Some sort of creature had waded ashore and was climbing the steep bank. Gorman saw it at the same time. Both men dropped their fishing rods, raced to their pickup truck, and turned on the headlights. There was nothing whatsoever to be seen. The creature had simply faded away into the night.

"What in the heck do you suppose that was?" gasped Johnson, his voice hoarse with excitement.

"Beats me." Gorman shook his head. "It looked like an ape, but apes don't get that big. Besides, what would an ape be doing around here anyway?"

"How about a bear?" inquired Johnson, "Would a bear cross a river and walk up a bank on his hind legs?"

"That was definitely not a bear. I don't know what it was, but it wasn't a bear." Gorman made a gesture with his hand. "Come on," he said. "Let's have a look around and see if we can see anything."

They spent the next fifteen minutes driving slowly back and forth along the river. Johnson had a spotlight on his truck, and he shined it in all directions. "I wonder just what the heck that thing could have been," he kept muttering to himself.

"Do you suppose it could have been something that escaped from a zoo or circus somewhere?" his partner asked at one point.

"I've never seen anything in a zoo or circus that looked like that thing," Johnson told him.

The search produced nothing, and they drove back to the place where they had been fishing. They found the tracks with no trouble, but they were merely shapeless depressions in the sand.

"I know that wasn't a man we saw," Johnson said thoughtfully, "but it climbed up that bank just like a man would. It was bending forward and digging in with its toes. A man goes up a steep bank the same way."

"Let's get out of here." Gorman was understandably nervous. "That thing might decide to come back, and I don't want to be around if it does."

"Do you think we ought to drive into town and report this?" Johnson asked when they were back in the truck.

"Not on your life," snorted Gorman. "People would think we were stark raving mad if we said we had seen a monster wade across the river and climb up the bank. I don't know about you, but I'm keeping my mouth shut. I don't want people to think I'm nuts."

"I suppose you're right," said Johnson.

The two men said nothing about their experience until reports of other sightings appeared in the local papers.

A dairy farmer named Wendorff was probably the next man to see the monster. His dogs began barking furiously early one morning. All three of them were on the porch, and it seemed as though they wanted to come into the house. This was a peculiar situation. The dogs were never allowed inside the house, and they only barked when they were bringing the cows home.

Wendorff glanced at his alarm clock. He always got up at five o'clock, and it was nearly that time now. There was no sense in

staying in bed any longer. His wife and daughter always slept until six-thirty, however, so he dressed quickly and went outside to quiet the dogs.

It was immediately apparent that everything was not as it should be. The dogs almost knocked him down when he opened the kitchen door. They were quivering with fear, and one of them had been sick on the porch. Not a breath of air stirred, and the farmer detected a peculiar odor. It smelled as though someone had been shooting off firecrackers.

Then the farmer noticed something even more peculiar. A dark figure was heading across a field in the direction of the river. It walked with an odd, shuffling gait. It looked rather like a very large old man wearing a fur overcoat, he thought. It was still not fully light, and the figure was over two hundred meters away, but Wendorff found it impossible to believe that it was a man he was looking at.

On an impulse he dashed inside for his rifle. The thing had trespassed on his property and frightened his dogs. If he fired a couple of shots over its head, it would think twice before coming back.

His wife was sitting up in bed when he went to the closet for some shells. "What are you doing with the gun?" she asked.

"There's something out there," he said, jerking open a drawer.

"What sort of something?"

Wendorff said, "I don't know."

"What's wrong with the dogs?" she asked next.

"I don't know. Something scared them, I guess." The farmer found the shells and went back out onto the porch. There was nothing to be seen. The creature had disappeared completely.

The sun was nearly overhead before Wendorff found time to do some detective work. There were no signs of anything around the house or farm buildings, so he drove down to the river to have a look. His luck was a bit better there. A set of tracks led down to

the water, but it was impossible to tell what sort of a creature had made them.

It was also impossible to describe the creature he had seen. When questioned by his wife, he merely shrugged his shoulders and said he guessed it looked like something part way between a great big man in a fur overcoat, a bear walking on its hind legs, and a sort of gorillalike thing.

This was the same description that Wendorff later gave reporters. Like Johnson and Gorman, he didn't report his experience until other people said that they had seen a monster.

MOMO MAKES THE

HE

Lorem ipsum dolo
nonnumy eiusmo
erat volupat. Ut
ut aliquip ex ea
in reprehender
dolore eu fug
dignissim qu
molestias e

ADLINES

tur adipiscing elit, sed diam zum
it labore et dolore magna aliqua
am, quis nostrud exercitation nisi
t. Duis autem vel eum irure dolor
sse molestaie consequat, vel illum
ero eos et accusam et iusto odiom
itum delenit aigue duos dolor et se
ipiditat non provident, simil sunt it
im id est laborum et dolor fuga. Et
it distinct. Nam liber tempor cumet
ing in quodmaxit

potest fier ad augendas cum conscient to factor tum
Et tamen in busdam neque pecun modut est neque n
libiding gen epular religuard cupiditat, quas nulla p
Improb pary minuit, potius inflammad ut coercend
videantur. Invitat igitur vera ratio bene sanos ad iu
fidem. Neque hominy infant aut iniuste fact est co
efficerd possit duo contenud notiner si effecerit, et
ingen liberalitat magis conveniunt, da but tuntung
et, aptissim est ad quiet. Endium caritat praesert
caus peccand quaert en imigent cupidat a natura
sine julla inura autend inanc sunt is parend non e
Concupis plusque in inspinuria detriment est qua

It was a hot summer afternoon in 1972, and eight-year-old Terry Harrison was playing alone in the back yard. His play was suddenly interrupted by a series of deep growls. Terry glanced around him—and his eyes opened wide in terror. The growls were coming from a giant creature covered with shaggy black hair. The boy stared in terrified fascination for a few seconds, then raced for the house. He had seen enough.

Doris Harrison, Terry's sister, was a pretty and intelligent girl of fifteen. She took one look at her brother's ashen face and knew at once that he'd had a terrible fright. "What's wrong, Terry?" she asked. "What happened?"

"Out there," the boy stammered. "There's a monster or something out there."

Doris looked out the kitchen window and gasped. A huge hairy creature was shuffling up the hill behind their house. It appeared to be about seven feet (2.12 m) tall. Its head was shaped like a pumpkin and covered with shaggy black hair. "Lock the doors, Terry," she said to her brother. "I'm going to call Mom and Dad."

Edgar Harrison rushed straight home from his café in Louisiana, Missouri. He found his son and daughter almost hysterical with fear. The story they blurted out didn't really make much sense to him, though. The age of monsters had ended long, long ago. His children had most likely seen a large black bear.

"No, it wasn't a bear, Daddy," Terry insisted. "It was like a—a—a—"

"Like a gorilla," Doris said. "Only—only—" Like her brother, the girl couldn't find the right words to describe the creature they had seen.

His children had seen something out of the ordinary. Edgar Harrison was absolutely convinced of that. But what was it that they had seen? What sort of a creature was it that had frightened them so terribly? Both of them insisted that it wasn't a bear, so it had to be something else. Harrison decided to find out for himself. He ordered his son and daughter to stay indoors, then took his rifle and started up the hill.

Marzolf Hill lies on the western end of a large wooded area surrounded by farmland. It is roughly triangular in shape and is bordered by the Mississippi and Cuivre rivers. Limestone caves abound in the area, and so do poisonous snakes. Bear, deer, and wild pigs are seen there from time to time. And a monster may have been seen there in the summer of 1972.

Only two things of interest were found by Harrison. An area of grass had been trampled flat near the top of the hill. He could only guess, of course, but it seemed that some heavy creature had been stamping back and forth while looking down at his house. The other interesting thing was a bush. A few green leaves still remained, but the others had been pulled off. What had happened to them? he wondered. Had the monster pulled them off and eaten them?

Harrison was still studying the bush when he heard a deep-throated growl that went on for several seconds. A piercing scream followed. The sounds seemed to be coming from far away, but they were still much too close for comfort. The café owner gripped his rifle tightly and hurried down the hill. As soon as he got home, he phoned the Louisiana police station.

Louisiana Police Chief Shelby Ward arrived in a matter of minutes. He was accompanied by Gus Artus, a state conservation department wildlife official, and a reporter from the Louisiana *Press-Journal*. After talking to the Harrison children, the three men were certain that Terry and Doris were perfectly sincere. Something had scared them out of their wits.

The police chief's mind raced wildly. He had been receiving strange reports for the last few weeks. Farmers had complained that their gardens and orchards had been raided and that something—or someone—had been frightening their livestock. A few said that they had heard growls and screams at night. Could it be, then, that the creature seen by the Harrison children was responsible for all these incidents? Ward asked himself.

It was too late to do any exploring on Marzolf Hill that night. The story of the Harrison children's experience, however, made the front page of the *Press-Journal* the next day, and the monster reports began to pour in.

Although most of the calls were obviously sincere, a few were ridiculous reports phoned in by practical jokers and publicity-seeking crackpots. One man told Chief Ward that he had seen Momo cross Highway 79 with a sheep in its mouth. Another said that a hairy monster at least ten feet (3.03 m) tall had leaped at him from a tree. And still others reported that giants with glowing red eyes had stared at them out of the darkness.

Poor Police Chief Ward had his hands full. Reports kept coming in, and the majority of them had to be investigated. To his surprise, literally hundreds of people in the Louisiana area claimed that they had heard frightening growls and piercing screams. At least a dozen reliable citizens insisted that they had seen a creature similar to the one seen by Terry and Doris Harrison.

About a week after Momo had made such a big splash in the newspapers, two men barged into the Louisiana police station. They had been fishing in the Cuivre River, they told Chief Ward, and they had seen the monster. It had been only about one hundred fifty feet (45.5 m) from them. It was wading across the river. The water was nearly six feet (1.83 m) deep at that spot which meant that Momo was well over seven feet (2.12 m) tall. As soon as the monster saw them, it began to run in the opposite direction.

Ward had known the two men for many years. Both of them were perfectly reliable. If they said that they had seen Momo, then it was safe to assume that they actually had seen some unfamiliar creature. "Let's go have a look," he said.

It was obvious that the men had left in a hurry. All of their fishing equipment was still lying on the bank. "It must have come out of the river right about there," one of the men said, pointing upstream.

The tracks they found in the sand told a strange story. They were difficult to read, but the men were certain that the creature that had made them had only three toes. The story didn't end there, though. Smaller tracks were found a bit farther up the river. Momo, it seemed, had either a son or a daughter or a companion much smaller than it was.

Shelby Ward did some hard thinking. Doris Harrison, he suddenly remembered, had told him that the creature had picked something up in his arms as he climbed up Marzolf Hill. Could that something have been a smaller monster? he wondered. The second set of tracks were less than half the size of those coming out of the river, so it certainly seemed possible. This discovery did absolutely nothing for the police chief's morale. Instead of having only one monster to worry about, he might now have two of them on his hands.

It was not a very happy police chief who went back to the station that night to file his report.

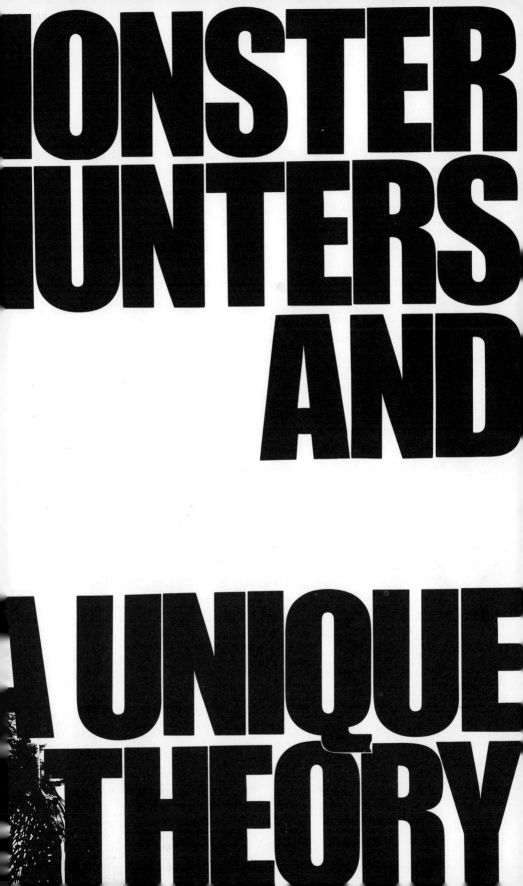

MONSTER
HUNTERS
AND

A UNIQUE
THEORY

As far as Police Chief Ward was concerned, the monster hunters were a greater menace than Momo. The creature had become big news, and armed men en masse came roaring into the peaceful community in Pike County. Some came from as far away as Texas and Ohio.

The result was bedlam. Hunters tramped across fields and through gardens and orchards. Gates and fences were broken down, and crops were trampled underfoot. Shots rang out at all hours, and two men swore that they had shot a monster which had immediately sunk to the bottom of the Cuivre River.

Shelby Ward knew that drastic action had to be taken. One of Wendorff's bulls had been mistaken for the monster one night and shot dead. The next victim might be a human. There were other dangers as well: a person unfamiliar with the wooded terrain could easily get lost. Marzolf and the surrounding hills were honeycombed with caves, and rattlesnakes were common. Something had to be done to protect these people from themselves, so the police chief placed a warning in the *Press-Journal*. No one with a gun would be allowed on Marzolf Hill, he said. Then he went a step further. Trespassing was against the law, he warned, and anyone found guilty of this offense would be either arrested or fined.

In the same issue of the paper, he tried to calm the fears of the residents of Pike County. "We have no reason to think that the creature is dangerous," he said. "If people are frightened, however, they should stay inside their homes and keep their doors locked. If something comes around their houses, they have plenty of time to call the police or a neighbor. They can also defend themselves from inside their houses, if necessary."

Not everyone took Momo seriously, of course. Some people looked upon the entire business as a huge joke. A few of the skeptics, though, suddenly found themselves firm believers. Ellis Minor was one of them.

Minor was an experienced outdoorsman who lived in an isolated area near the Mississippi River. He was returning home one afternoon when he saw something standing at the edge of a clearing. Although it was still broad daylight, he couldn't believe his eyes. He had always pooh-poohed the monster stories. There couldn't possibly be such a creature in Pike County, he'd insisted, and now he was seeing it himself. "I'm not laughing at those Momo stories anymore," he told Shelby Ward. "I've seen the thing myself, and it sure made a believer out of me."

"It was no more than one hundred twenty-five yards [37.91 m] from me, and I had a good look," Minor went on. "I couldn't see its eyes or its face, but it had coal black hair nearly down to its chest. I'd guess it was pretty close to nine feet tall and real broad across the shoulders. Everything about it was real big and scary. The second I stopped the pickup, it took off for the woods and disappeared." Then he said again, "Man, that thing sure made a believer out of me!"

"Did the thing make any sounds?" Ward wanted to know.

"Not when I saw it," replied Minor, "but I heard them a few minutes later. The thing screamed like a woman would scream if someone attacked her on a dark night. It made shivers run up and down my spine."

Strangely enough, a woman's screams apparently gave Momo a bad fright. A Louisiana housewife who refused to let the *Press-Journal* use her name told a reporter that she had parked on a lonely road near Cuivre River State Park and walked into the woods to pick wild flowers. When she returned, Momo was standing just a few feet from her car. "I had always laughed at those monster stories," she said, "but that thing was for real, and I'm not kidding. I screamed so loud that they must have heard me in Booneville. The monster loped off toward the river," she continued, "and I ran for the car. I was shaking so bad, though, that it took me about five minutes to unlock the door."

Kim Sexton of the Independence *Examiner* was another skeptic who became a believer. She drove over to Louisiana to get material for a humorous article on the monster. To her surprise, she learned that Momo was no laughing matter. Many of the people she talked to were genuinely worried.

"I believe those I talked with really did see and hear something unusual," she reported. "These were men and women of high character who did not seem to exaggerate or to seek publicity. Most of them convinced me there is something in those hills of Pike County that is strange to our country. It wasn't so much what they said that convinced me. It was the way they said it."

Momo dropped out of the news in the late fall of 1972. There were no more sightings and no more piercing screams in the night. The creature disappeared as suddenly as it had appeared. Some people thought that it might be hiding in one of the numerous caves in the area, but two men had a theory uniquely their own. They were Daniel Garcia and Hayden Hewes of the International Unidentified Flying Object Bureau in Oklahoma City.

Garcia and Hewes told Louisiana Police Chief Shelby Ward that the unidentified monster could have come from an unidentified flying object. An unusually large number of flying saucers had been seen in Pike County that summer, they said, and Momo may actually have been a visitor from another planet. An advanced civilization in space may have put it down in Missouri so that it could see what things were like here on Earth. It had done what it had come here to do, so it had probably gone back to wherever it was that it had come from.

Chief Ward merely shrugged his shoulders. Between flying saucers and monsters, he had had a hectic summer. If Momo had left Pike County in a flying saucer, that was its business. The fact that the creature had apparently left his district was the important thing, and he didn't really care where it had gone. There was nothing he could do about the unidentified flying objects, but the unidentified monster had made an awful nuisance of itself.

THAT "THING" IN THE

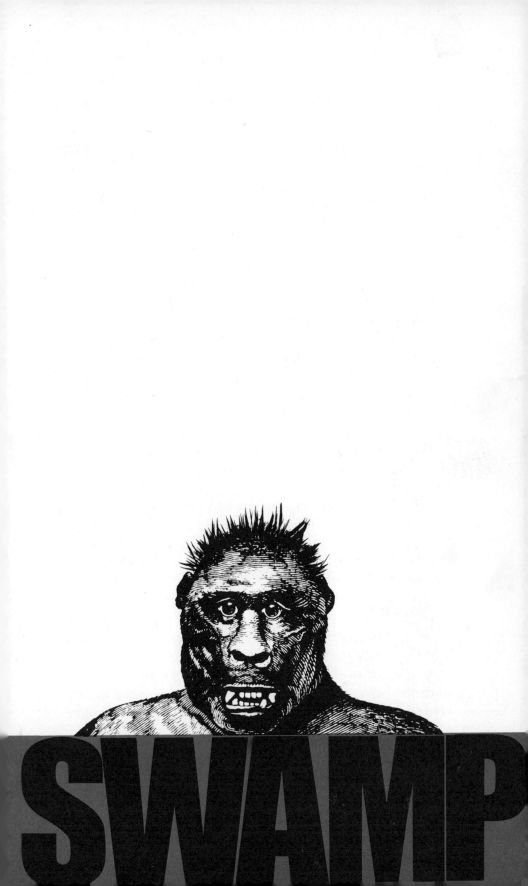

The Honey Island Swamp Monster has received far less publicity than any of the other unidentified creatures on our continent. This isn't really too surprising. The swamp is almost as frightening as the monster itself. Weekend adventurers usually avoid the place, and those familiar with the area treat it with great respect.

Although the swamp is no more than a two-hour drive from New Orleans, it lies in an entirely different world. This is bayou country. Sluggish waterways twist and turn through forests of huge cypress trees draped heavily with Spanish moss. Alligators and poisonous snakes abound. The bird life is fantastic, and the frog population is said to be the densest in the world. Bear, deer, and wild boar can sometimes be found on the larger islands. The fishing is excellent, but a careless or inexperienced fisherman could soon be lost in the trackless area. Residents of St. Tammany Parish seem to enjoy telling visitors about people who have gone off into the swamp and never been seen again.

There have always been interesting stories about Honey Island Swamp. During the old pirate days it was a hideout for outlaws. Legends say that millions of dollars in gold and other valuables are hidden there. One authority says that small boats loaded with plunder were sunk in the bayous that wind through the vine- and moss-draped forest. A chest full of treasure was found in the swamp in the 1940s, so there is every reason to think that the legends are founded on fact.

The state of Louisiana plans to make the forty-seven-thousand-acre (19,020.64 hectares) swamp into a state park at some time in the near future. It is a savagely beautiful place and will be a lovely retreat for people from the nearby cities. Picnic areas, camp grounds, and hunting and fishing lodges are to be built along the bayous. Much of the area will be signposted to help keep people from getting lost. The more timid will be able to hire a guide to take them through the trackless maze of waterways.

People who come to the park will all have one thing in com-

mon. All of them will come hoping to see the Honey Island
Swamp Monster.

Frank Davis first heard about the Honey Island Swamp Monster in 1973. The story intrigued him, and he set out to see what
he could learn.

Davis was in a good position for gathering information. He
was employed by the Louisiana Wildlife and Fisheries Commis-
sion. He had been born and raised in Slidell, a town on the edge
of Honey Island Swamp. Many of his friends fished and hunted
there. Some of them had seen the monster. They were quite willing to talk about their experiences, but they refused to let Davis
use their names. "I don't want people to think I'm a kook," one
told him. Everyone in Slidell knew that Frank Davis was also a
free-lance writer, and they didn't want their names associated
with the monster.

Fortunately, one man was willing to risk ridicule. His name is
Harlan Ford, and he is a lifelong resident of Slidell, Louisiana.

Few people know the Honey Island Swamp better than Harlan
Ford. He is an expert woodsman who has run trap lines, hunted,
and fished throughout the entire area. It was while hunting with
a friend that he first came face to face with the monster.

The two men were hunting on Honey Island itself. They were
on a virtually unexplored part of the island. Ford says he doubts
seriously that more than a dozen men have ever been in that
section. The vegetation was so dense that they practically had to
fight their way forward.

Finally, they broke through into a small clearing. "That's
when we saw the thing," Ford recalls. "It must have heard us
thrashing through the brush, but it was standing with its back to
us. We both stood and stared. Neither of us had ever seen anything like it before, and we had trouble believing our eyes.

"Then the thing turned around and looked at us," he went on. "It was ugly and sinister. Sort of like something out of a horror movie. I'm sure it was at least seven feet [2.12 m] tall and it must have weighed four hundred pounds [181.44 kg]. The hair on the head hung down about two feet [.60 m]. The rest of it was covered with short, dingy, gray hair. Its chest and shoulders were massive. The face was square and mean, and I could see two rows of teeth in the powerful jaws. The thing must have stood staring at us for a full minute before it went tearing off into the woods."

Ford admits that the monster gave him a bad scare. He had seen something completely different, and he couldn't explain it. Neither could he get it off his mind. There was some sort of strange creature out there in the Honey Island Swamp, and he was determined to learn more about the "whatever-it-was."

For the next couple of weeks, Harlan Ford made almost daily treks out to the place where he had seen the monster. Although he always carried his rifle, he sincerely hoped that he wouldn't have to use it. A plan was beginning to take shape in his mind. If he could find a place which the creature frequented regularly, he might be able to lure it into a trap.

Before Ford could get his trap ready, he walked into a trap himself. He still isn't quite sure how it happened. Like many men who spend a lot of time alone, he's a man of few words. Publicity is just about the last thing he wants. The story of his experience with the monster had been written up in the newspapers, however, and a television director contacted him at his home in Slidell. Before Ford realized it, he had accepted an invitation to appear on WVUE-TV in New Orleans.

No one who saw the program could possibly doubt his complete sincerity. They all recognized the fact that this was not the kind of man to dream up a tall tale. Ford was an outdoorsman— a man who was far more comfortable in a swamp than he was in a television studio. It was obvious that he wasn't there to impress anybody.

Ford told his story in a simple and straightforward manner. He showed the audience plaster of Paris casts he had made of the creature's tracks and said he believed that there were several such creatures in the swamp. The monster he had seen, he felt, was not related in any way to the well-known Bigfoot, or the Fouke Monster. When asked if the monster had frightened him, Ford forthrightly said, "Yes. It scared me real bad."

Shortly after Ford had appeared on the television program, the *St. Bernard* (Louisiana) *News* published an article about his experience. It was headlined "The Monster of Honey Island Swamp" and was illustrated with pictures of Ford and the plaster casts he had made of the creature's tracks. A zoologist at Louisiana State University read the article and arranged to meet Ford.

The zoologist was understandably confused. He believed Ford's story, and he knew that the casts couldn't very well tell a lie. He knew, too, that creatures which were most likely similar had reportedly been seen in Mississippi, Georgia, and the Florida Everglades.

Ford had always said that the monster left three-toed tracks behind it. The scientist, however, wasn't sure. He pointed to a stubby knob slightly lower than the toes and expressed the opinion that this could be a fourth appendage. "But even if it is," he said to Ford, "we still don't know what sort of a creature it was that made these tracks."

"This whole business of the Honey Island Swamp Monster is a complete mystery to me," the zoologist was quoted as saying in the *St. Bernard News* on October 29, 1975. "The creature could be a mutant of some sort or simply an animal we haven't discovered yet. That doesn't sound very scientific, I know, but it's the only answer I have."

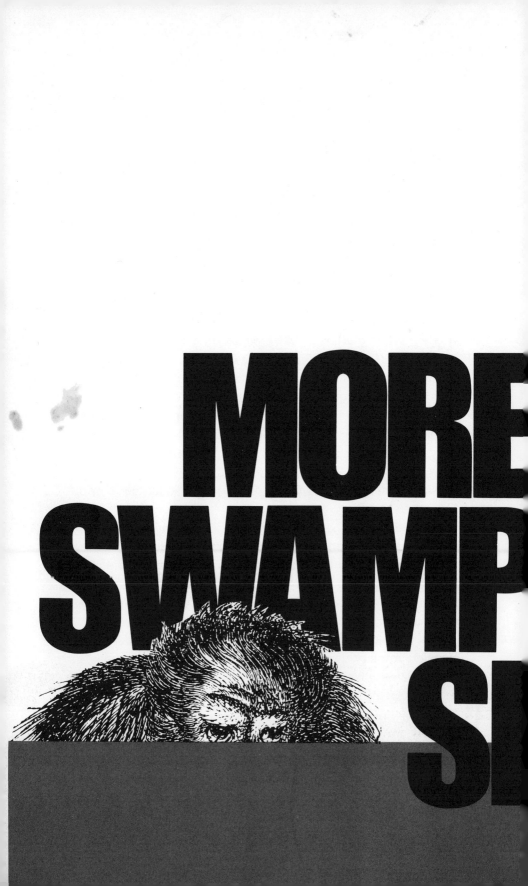

Harlan Ford will not tell anyone exactly where he saw the Honey Island Swamp Monster. He believes that the creature could be dangerous if it were pursued and he's afraid that someone could get hurt. "If that happened," he says, "I'd feel responsible."

Frank Davis, however, thinks that the creature ranges far and wide throughout the entire swamp area. He has talked to people who claim to have seen it in the Pearl River, Lake Borgne, and other places in the swamp. Ford agrees that this might very well be true, but he still feels that the monster spends most of its time in one particular area.

In the summer of 1973 three men returned to Covington, Louisiana, with a very strange story. They had been camped out while fishing on the Pearl River and were relaxing around the fire late one evening. For no reason that they could understand, they began to feel uneasy. Although they had heard nothing out of the ordinary, they sensed that they were no longer alone. They all felt as though someone—or something—was watching them.

It was an eerie sensation. The river flowed along silently. The only sounds were the croaking of frogs and the occasional hoot of an owl. A large yellow moon cast its shadow on the water. It should have been a scene of perfect peace, but it wasn't. The men were so tense that they spoke only in hushed tones.

Finally, one of them picked up a flashlight and hatchet and got to his feet. "I'm going to have a look around," he said. "I've got the feeling that there's something funny going on around here, and I want to find out what it is."

"You're chasing spooks," said one of the others.

"I don't care what I'm chasing, as long as I chase it away," was the reply.

The man had gone no more than twenty yards (6.06 m) from the campsite when something suddenly began crashing through the brush in front of him. In the beam of his flashlight, he was able to see a large, hairy form rushing toward the river. "Hey!" he yelled to his companions. "Hey, look at that thing!" The other two men reached the bank just in time to see a strange two-legged monster splash into the water and disappear.

The three fishermen were in an unhappy situation. They didn't like the idea of trying to find their way out of the swamp at night. Neither did they like the idea of staying where they were. Their visitor might decide to return, and a hatchet was their only protection.

After a discussion they decided that getting lost was the lesser of the two dangers. Everything was quickly stashed back in the boat, and the fishermen set off for home. They had seen enough of the Honey Island Swamp to last them for a long time.

A fishing guide and his client also met the monster on the Pearl River. They were chugging slowly upstream through the swamp when the boat struck a submerged object. The guide thought it might have been an alligator or a turtle. He stopped to have a look, but he couldn't see a thing. His companion, however, suddenly jumped up and pointed toward shore.

The guide saw the creature immediately. It was scrambling swiftly out of the water. Once it reached the bank, it immediately raced off on two legs and disappeared into the swamp.

Although the two men had seen the monster at exactly the same time, their descriptions varied in certain details. The guide thought that the creature was about five feet (1.51 m) tall and covered with short, grayish fur or hair. The fisherman believed the height to be close to seven feet (2.12 m). He was also of the opinion that the body was covered with skin. Both of the men agreed, however, that the scalp hair was long and shaggy and that the creature was massively built.

The difference in descriptions is easily understood. A man who sees a monster is bound to get excited. His eyes will be popping out and he may miss or misinterpret certain details. This, of course, makes the job more difficult for serious researchers like Frank Davis and Paul Serpas of the *St. Bernard News.* They have talked to over a dozen men—and two women—who claim to have seen the monster, but they still don't know exactly what it looks like.

Davis has been told that the casts made by Harlan Ford were sent to Washington's Smithsonian Institution. Scientists there studied them and found no evidence of a hoax. A number of zoologists and anthropologists from Louisiana universities said the same thing.

One even went a step farther. He said that the tracks were not so unusual that they couldn't be believed. It was possible, he went on, that there was a type of animal living in the vast wilderness of the swamp which was still unknown to man.

Paul Serpas made an interesting observation and asked an interesting question in one of his articles in the *St. Bernard News.* It reads:

At a recent convention of the American Anthropological Association, an ancient carved stone head, representing an unknown type of animal, was displayed. The carving is remarkably similar to the descriptions generally given of the Honey Island Swamp Monster. Could it be, then, that such creatures were known hundreds or even thousands of years ago, but have managed to go undetected by modern science?

That is a question that we would all love to have answered for us.

THE LAKE WORTH
STER

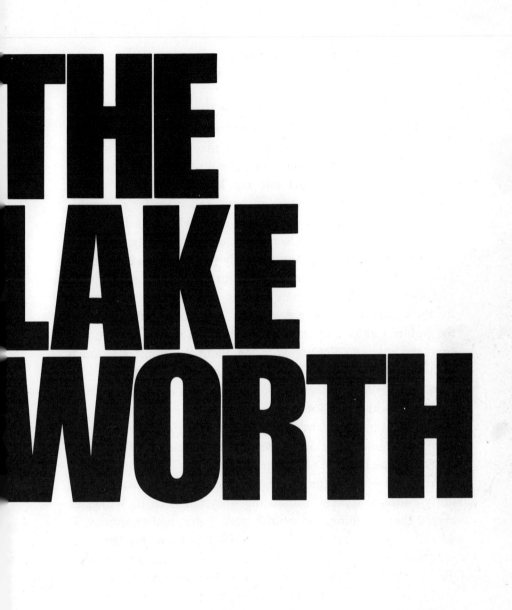

It was a front-page article in the Fort Worth *Star-Telegram* of July 10, 1969 that set off the biggest monster hunt in Texas history. Six people told the police that they had seen a strange "something" near Greer Island in Lake Worth. The creature was about seven feet (2.12 m) tall and looked rather like a goat running on its hind legs. Short, dirty-white hair or fur covered it from top to bottom. The people had obviously had a bad scare, and the police were forced to take the matter seriously.

The matter was also taken seriously by dozens and dozens of Fort Worth residents. They rushed out to the lake armed with everything from baseball bats to rifles. There was a monster on the loose, and it had to be destroyed. The fact that the area was the Nature Center and Game Reserve doesn't seem to have discouraged anyone. "I'm not worrying about the monster as much as I am about all those people wandering around out there with guns," said Police Sergeant A. J. Hudson. "I'm afraid somebody's going to get himself shot."

The creature made front-page news again on the following day. A headline in the *Star-Telegram* proclaimed. "Police, Residents Observe but Can't Identify 'Monster'."

Although none of the police actually saw the monster, about thirty curiosity seekers insisted that they had seen it. Witnesses agreed that the thing was whitish gray, hairy, and enormous. It walked like a man, they said, but it definitely wasn't human.

Rumors spread like wildfire. One said that a farmer had seen the thing run off with his dog under its arm. Another farmer had found three sheep dead in his pasture. Their necks had been broken, and all three of them had been partially eaten. A fisherman on Lake Worth had supposedly had his stringer of fish stolen by the monster. Several people had been treated for shock in a Fort Worth hospital after a monster had jumped out of a tree onto their car. The monster had kidnapped the wife of a young couple living near the lake. It had also kidnapped a farmer's teen-age daughter. Cars were its worst enemy, however, and it had turned several of them completely over, smashed windows on a number of others, and ripped the fenders and bumpers off several more. There was even a rumor that four policemen had raced for the safety of their patrol cars when they heard the monster scream late one night on the shore of Lake Worth.

Whether it existed or not, the police looked upon the Lake Worth Monster as a serious menace. The creature had received a lot of publicity on the radio and in the local papers, and it seemed that half of the city was out hunting it. There are several picnic areas on the shore of the lake, and all of them were crammed with cars belonging to monster hunters. "I'd guess that there are somewhere between two hundred and two hundred fifty people out there beating the bushes," a police officer told a *Star-Telegram* reporter, "and most of them are inexperienced kids who will shoot at anything that moves."

The policeman proved to be right. Just a few hours later, a seventeen-year-old boy was shot in the shoulder with a deer rifle. He was six feet four inches (1.93 m) tall. He was wearing white coveralls at the time, and a trigger-happy hunter mistook him for the Lake Worth Monster.

That did it! The Fort Worth Police Department immediately made it an offense to carry firearms in the Nature Center and Game Reserve. Anyone found guilty of doing so would be liable to a fine of up to $200.

No more guns were brought into the area after that, but the monster hunters came armed with just about everything else. "I've never seen so many knives, swords, tire tools, chains, clubs, and other weapons of every kind in one place in my life," moaned Patrolman James McGee. "There's even one idiot out there with only a lasso. He says he's going to capture the thing, then sell it to the Forest Park Zoo for a million dollars."

One person, at least, doesn't seem to have taken the monster very seriously. At one of the entrances to the Nature Center and Game Reserve, he put up a large sign saying Lake Worth Monster Season Now Open—Males Only.

The most enthusiastic monster hunter of them all is a Fort

Worth housewife by the name of Sallie Ann Clarke. She says that she saw the creature four times in 1969, and she says it very convincingly. Although the monster has supposedly not been seen since that summer, Sallie Ann drives out to Lake Worth occasionally. She doesn't know what has happened to it, but she's firmly convinced that she'll see it again sometime.

In the beginning Sallie Ann looked upon the monster as a huge joke. The radio broadcasts and newspaper articles amused her. While it was true that there was a lot of wilderness area around the lake, she couldn't believe that a monster had made the area its home. Where had the thing come from, she wondered, and why had it never been seen before? Had the thing suddenly dropped out of the sky or what?

It was perhaps more of a whim than anything else that prompted Sallie Ann to drive out to Lake Worth one swelteringly hot July evening. To her amazement, there were cars parked everywhere. People were milling around all over the place. So many flashlights flickered from the bushes that it looked like an army of fireflies.

"What's going on around here?" Sallie Ann finally asked a policeman. "Are all those people hunting the monster?"

"They're all nuts." The policeman was plainly unhappy.

"Do you really believe there's such a thing as the Lake Worth Monster?" she inquired.

"Look, lady, I'm only a dumb cop," the policeman said, making a gesture with both hands. "I only do what I'm told to do, and I only know what I read in the newspapers."

"But it said in the *Star-Telegram* that—"

"Yeah, lady, I read that, too." The officer pushed back his cap, then added, "You don't have to believe everything you read in the newspapers, you know, lady."

Sallie Ann Clarke, however, became a firm believer in the Lake Worth Monster before the night was over.

NTASY?

It was very late when Sallie Ann got into her car and headed for home. She was tired and confused. The last few hours had been spent talking to people, and she didn't know what to think. Common sense told her that there could not possibly be a monster roaming around in the twentieth century. And even if there were, she reasoned, it certainly wouldn't make its home so close to a large city like Fort Worth. It would live in a place like the Florida Everglades or the great forests of the Pacific Northwest.

Then had all of those people lied to her? she asked herself. Several of them swore that they had heard a piercing scream that could not have been human. Two men, Ronnie Armstrong and Jim Stephens, insisted that they had seen a creature running through the brush on two legs. It was big and heavy and was covered with dirty-white fur. The creature was much too large to be either a man or an ape, so it had to be something else.

Mrs. Clarke was still searching for sensible answers when the totally unexpected happened. A huge whitish form suddenly emerged from a ditch as she was approaching the Lake Worth Bridge. It ran across the road and immediately disappeared into the brush on the far side. Although she only saw it for two or three seconds, she is absolutely convinced that she knows what it was. "I saw the Lake Worth Monster, and nobody can tell me otherwise," she says. "That's the only thing it could possibly have been."

And she could just possibly be right.

The reported sighting that hot July night in 1969 was a major event in the life of Sallie Ann Clarke. It brought on an acute case of monstermania. Much of her spare time was spent out at Lake Worth. She became a familiar figure to the other monster hunters as she trudged doggedly through the brush armed with her camera, notepad, and tape recorder.

Not only the monster hunters were interviewed, however. Sallie Ann talked to people who lived near the lake, and she went through old newspaper files and the archives. Monsters, she learned, were not new to Texas. They had reportedly been seen there as early as the 1700s and as recently as 1941. An Indian chief in Livingstone said that according to their legends there had *always* been monsters around Lake Worth.

But what kind of creatures were they? Sallie Ann wanted an answer to that question, and she thought she might be able to get it. The scientists in Fort Worth hadn't given her much help, so she decided to try someone who wasn't a scientist. She had read about John Green while doing her research. Green is Canada's foremost monster investigator. His chief interest is Bigfoot. The Lake Worth Monster may not have been a Bigfoot, she reasoned, but Green might be able to give her some clue as to its identity.

Green must have been impressed with the Fort Worth housewife's sincerity. It's a long way from British Columbia to Texas, but the monster investigator felt that he had to make the trip. Whether or not he found the long journey worthwhile is something we don't know.

The Canadian is an extremely cautious man. He has been gathering information on monsters for nearly twenty years. It's highly unlikely that anyone on the North American continent knows more about unidentified creatures than he does. He devotes all of his time to studying them and will travel almost anywhere to get more information. He will patiently listen to anyone, but he never ever makes wild guesses.

Although the Lake Worth Monster intrigued Green, he had to admit that he didn't know what it was. He did, however, know what it wasn't. It wasn't a Bigfoot, and he was willing to take bets on that. Both creatures were very large. Both ran on two legs, and there the similarities ended. "They're probably not even distant cousins," Green concluded.

The summer of 1969 simmered on. Reports of sightings kept coming in, but the monster seldom made the front page of the

Fort Worth newspapers. The original flurry of excitement had died down. Even some of the most enthusiastic hunters had put their weapons away. Instead of chasing after the monster, they were now chasing after other things.

This doesn't mean, of course, that people had lost interest in the creature. Far from it. A play called *The Lake Worth Monster* drew record crowds when it was put on at the Casa Mañana Playhouse.

John Simons, the playwright, lived on the shore of the lake. He had never seen the monster, but he couldn't bear the thought of its being killed or harmed. "I feel sorry for the poor creature," he told a *Star-Telegram* reporter. "It's lonely and it's isolated and it must be terribly afraid. I don't know for sure whether it's real or unreal—a freak or an apparition. Anyway, that's not important. The point I want to make in my play is that the thing has not harmed anyone. It minds its own business. We should respect it—no matter what it is—and grant it the full protection of the law."

Before the opening night *The Lake Worth Monster* got some free publicity. The playwright had Sallie Ann Clark to thank for that. The Texas housewife managed to get a flash photo of the creature one night when some hunters chased it past the tree stump on which she was resting.

According to Sallie Ann, she had driven out to the Nature Center and Game Reserve after her evening meal. Several sightings had been reported in the last few days, and she hoped to get another glimpse of the monster. Actually, she did much better than that. Before the night was over, she had what she hoped would be a good picture of the thing she had been chasing for so long.

Unfortunately, the photograph doesn't really tell us very much at all. It shows a white, hairy "something-or-other" standing in some weeds. The back is to the camera, and there is no indication of movement. Neither is it possible to judge the height or weight accurately. Neither arms nor legs can be seen.

It's obvious, too, that the photo was taken at very close range. Sallie Ann says that she jumped off the stump and snapped the photo as the creature went tearing past her. "I honestly don't think that the thing was more than ten yards [9.14 m] from me when I took the picture," she declared.

Dick Pratt, the naturalist at the Nature Center and Game Reserve, is far from convinced that there is a monster in the area. "Personally, I don't think there's anything larger than a bobcat around here," he says. "I know that some large tracks have supposedly been found and that a lot of folks swear that they've seen a monster, but I find the whole business pretty hard to believe."

This isn't surprising. It *is* hard to believe that there's a monster cavorting around almost within sight of the lights of Fort Worth. It's also hard to believe that so many people would tell a pack of lies. The fact remains, too, that something did show up on Sallie Ann Clarke's photograph.

We don't know what that something was, but whatever it was, it was much too large to be a bobcat.

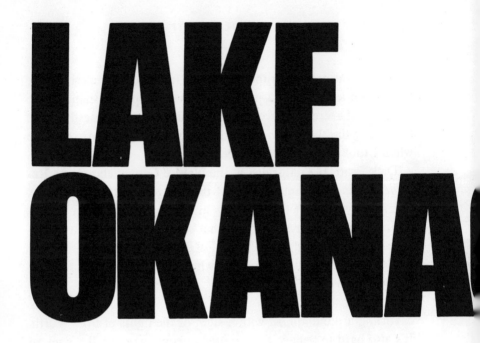

LAKE
OKANAC

"LOCH
NESS M

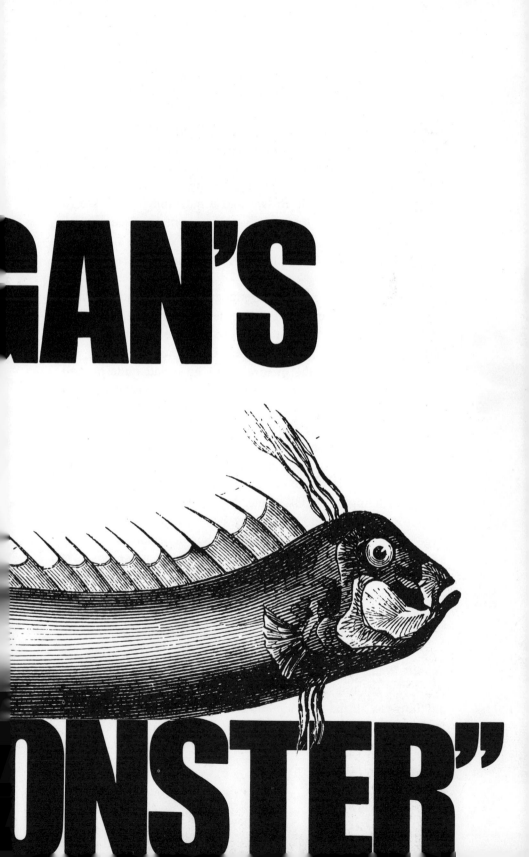

North America's most famous lake monster lives in Lake Okanagan. This beautiful body of water lies in Canada and is just a short distance north of the border between British Columbia and Washington State. The lake is sixty-nine miles (111.09 km) long and varies from one mile to two and a half miles (1.61 km to 4.02 km) in width. Its total area is roughly one hundred twenty-seven square miles (328.93 sq. km). The monster's name is Ogopogo. He is known in the Shushwap Indian legends, however, as Naitaka.

Nobody knows exactly what Ogopogo looks like, but drawings on cliffs near the lake probably give us a rough idea. The drawings were there when the first settlers came. The Indians said that they hadn't drawn them and that they didn't know who had.

Whoever *did* draw the pictures must have had quite a good look at the monster. The drawings show a head somewhat like a goat's, a long neck and a heavy snakelike body, flippers, and a short stubby tail. There are two elongated bumps on top of the head which some say are horns and others say are ears. The cliff drawings pretty much fit the descriptions given by some who have seen the monster in recent years.

Indians living in the Okanagan Valley had a very healthy respect for their lake monster. They believed that he lived in a large cave near what is now known as Squally Point. There was a rocky island just off the point where the monster liked to have his meals. Young braves who worked up enough courage to visit Monster's Island found bones and skins lying all around and the rocks spattered with blood.

The monster never had to worry about going hungry. Whenever an Indian paddled his canoe anywhere in the vicinity of Squally Point, he carried a gift along for the monster spirit of the lake. The gift might be a puppy, a duck, the leg of a deer, or anything else. If the monster was given something to eat, the man in the canoe would be safe from attack.

But woe to the person who neglected to bring a gift! An Indian legend told about a chief named Timbasket who came with his family to visit the Shushwap tribe in the Okanagan Valley. Timbasket laughed at the stories about the monster in the lake. "There ain't no such animal," he probably said in his native language.

One morning Timbasket decided to take his family for a canoe ride along the shore of the lake. The Shushwap people told him to take a gift along for the monster spirit and to be sure to stay well clear of Squally Point. Timbasket merely laughed. He didn't believe in monsters. Besides, he was a chief, and a monster wouldn't dare to attack him.

When the Shushwap medicine man realized that Chief Timbasket did not take the monster seriously, he did what he could to protect his visitor from harm. First, he painted some pictures on the canoe that he hoped would frighten the monster away. Then he put a large dog in the canoe and told the chief to push it overboard near Monster's Island. Finally, he asked Timbasket to keep well away from Squally Point.

The Shushwap who watched Timbasket paddle off with his family were deeply alarmed. Instead of heading well out into the lake, the chief was staying close to the shore. Unless he changed course, he would pass between Monster's Island and Squally Point. This was Naitaka's territory and by far the most dangerous part of the lake.

Chief Timbasket paddled stolidly on. The Shushwap on shore waited anxiously for him to sacrifice the dog to Naitaka, but he apparently had no intention of doing so. He didn't take the monster seriously, and he wasn't willing to waste a perfectly good dog.

The Shushwap hardly dared to breathe as the canoe drew abreast of the passage. They all feared the worst—and the worst happened! The calm surface of the lake suddenly foamed and frothed. Mountainous waves smashed against the rocks of Squally Point and Monster's Island. Naitaka was angry. He had been denied a gift. His thrashing tail showed his fury, and the spray flew high into the air.

In just a few seconds it was all over. The lake was once again calm and peaceful. Not even a ripple could be seen on the surface. There was one thing, though, that could be seen by everyone on the shore. Timbasket's canoe was floating upside down a short distance off Squally Point. The chief and his family were nowhere to be seen, but everyone knew what had happened to them.

Timbasket had refused to give the monster spirit a gift, and Naitaka had taken his revenge.

John McDougal, an early settler in the Okanagan Valley, was told about the monster spirit by the Indians. The rancher was fond of the Shushwap. He spent a lot of time with them, and he came to believe that there really was a huge creature of some kind in the lake. To stay on the safe side, he never went out in his canoe without a gift for Naitaka.

But one day he left home and completely forgot to take a gift. He was a bit worried, but he had to get across the lake with his horse. McDougal decided to trust his luck. The lake was just over a mile (1.61 km) wide at that point, and his horse was a good swimmer. After tieing the horse's bridle to the stern of the canoe, he began paddling toward the far side.

They ran into trouble some distance from Monster's Island. For no reason that McDougal could understand, the horse suddenly went wild with fear. Some unknown force seemed to be pulling it down into the water.

McDougal was scared stiff. The horse appeared to be drowning. If the horse went down, it might drag the canoe down with it. The rancher had to act quickly because he knew that he wouldn't be able to swim all the way back to the shore. His jackknife was in his pocket, and he swiftly whipped it out and cut the rope tied to the bridle. Just seconds later the unfortunate horse disappeared into the depths of Lake Okanagan.

The Indians said that the water devil had taken the horse. The other settlers said that the horse had simply panicked and drowned. They found the story of the monster pretty hard to believe. None of them had ever seen it, and they didn't pay very much attention to the Indians' legends.

Then, in 1852, one of the settlers saw the monster! Her name was Mrs. John Allison, and she watched the creature for several minutes from a hill near their cabin. Mrs. Allison had heard about John McDougal's experience. She had also heard about Naitaka from her Indian friends. It had never occurred to her, though, that there might actually be an unexplained something in the lake.

It was a stormy summer afternoon when Mrs. Allison climbed the hill. Her husband had crossed the lake to buy supplies from the store at Okanagan Mission. A sudden storm had come up. The wind was lashing the water, and she was worried about his safety. Lake Okanagan could be a very dangerous place in bad weather.

To Mrs. Allison's relief, the storm did not last long. The rain stopped and the wind died down. There was even a bit of sunshine filtering through the clouds. Visibility improved rapidly, and the pioneer woman saw what she first thought was a man in a canoe.

Although conditions were far from perfect, she soon realized that her first impression couldn't possibly be correct. A man could not paddle a canoe at such speed. Neither would anyone sit in the bow and paddle. Even more confusing was the fact that parts of the canoe seemed to be below the surface of the lake.

That was confusing enough, but there was more to come. While Mrs. Allison watched, the object suddenly sank beneath the waves. It was then she realized that she had seen Naitaka, the water devil of the Shushwap Indian legends.

Records for the nineteenth century are rather sketchy. The Okanagan Valley was very sparsely populated at that time, and communications were poor. A rancher who saw the monster might tell his family and friends about it, but he certainly wouldn't get on his horse and make the long journey into town to report what he had seen.

Sightings became more frequent as more people moved into the region. Communications also improved dramatically. By the turn of the century there was a road all the way around the lake, and newspapers were being published in Vernon, Kelowna, and Penticton. Any news of the monster was almost certain to make the front page.

Everyone in the Okanagan Valley has always been fond of the lake devil, so people were sincerely worried about an article which appeared in the *Morning Post* in 1914. The report had been given to the editor by Frank Buckland of Kelowna.

Mr. Buckland and several friends had been camped on a beach near Greata Ranch. One of the men was strolling along the shore when he noticed a peculiar stench. He thought it might be a dead fish, and he went to investigate. But it wasn't a dead fish he found! It was the rotting body of the strangest creature he had ever seen.

The man hurried back to camp and called the others. All of them stood staring in amazement. They had no idea what the thing could be. It was entirely unlike any creature they had ever heard about.

Although the carcass was badly decomposed, the men were still able to get a fairly accurate description. It was about six feet (1.83 m) long and weighed about four hundred pounds (181.44 kg). There was no sign of a neck. The round head appeared to be attached directly to the body. No ears were visible; the nose was stubby and the teeth resembled those of a dog. Silky, bluish gray hair four or five inches (10.16 cm or 12.70 cm) in length covered the head and body. The tail was short, broad, and flat. It had two ivorylike tusks. There was a flipper on each side, and each flipper had claws like an eagle's.

A shoulder blade, the tusks, and the claws were put on exhibit in Kelowna for a number of years. An amateur naturalist timidly suggested that the creature might be a manatee, or a sea cow, but this was probably a wild guess. Sea cows and manatees are found in the Caribbean and some South American rivers. It's highly unlikely, therefore, that any of them could have found their way to Lake Okanagan in British Columbia, Canada.

So what was it that Frank Buckland and his friends found on the beach? People who had seen the monster of the Shushwap Indian legends always described it as a huge creature anywhere from twenty to seventy feet (6.06 to 21.23 m) long. Could it be, then, that the men had found a baby monster that had died after being washed ashore?

We'll never know the answer to that question. Scientists in 1914 apparently weren't interested in Kelowna's monster exhibit. Nobody came to make a scientific study of the shoulder blade, tusks, and claws, and the whole lot was eventually thrown out.

Such a thing would never happen today, of course, but times have changed greatly since 1914.

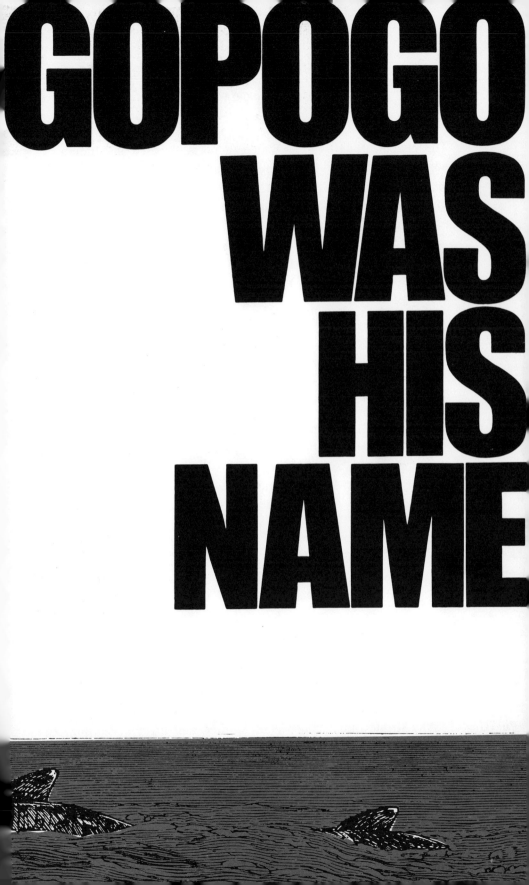

The people around Lake Okanagan normally used the Indian name Naitaka when they were discussing their monster. They also referred to it as the water demon, the water spirit, and that thing in the lake. Then, too, there were some who referred to it as a lot of foolishness.

In 1924 that thing in the lake was given a new name, and that name has become known throughout the world. A British entertainer was performing in Vernon on the northern tip of the lake in that year, and a verse from one of his songs went like this:

His mother was an insect,
His father was a whale.
A little bit of head,
And hardly any tail,
And Ogopogo was his name.

The words seemed to describe the Lake Okanagan Monster. It was just the sort of creature that would have an insect for a mother and a whale for a father. The drawings on the cliffs near the lake showed a monster with a small head and hardly any tail and that, too, described the water devil.

And so the Indian name Naitaka died that night in Vernon, British Columbia, and the monster has been known as Ogopogo ever since.

Not everyone is happy about that. The people in Kelowna, for example, felt that the people in Vernon had no right to give the creature a new name. It had been seen far more often around Kelowna, so it obviously thought that Kelowna was a much nicer place than Vernon.

Kelowna had to protect its interest in the monster, so it made Ogopogo an honorary citizen of the town. The next step was to erect a large statue of it in the park. Then, in 1970, the Ogopogo Serendipidity Society was founded by a group of Kelowna businessmen.

Like the Loch Ness Monster, Ogopogo's behavior is completely unpredictable. It will suddenly pop up in the most unexpected places at the most unexpected times. There might be a dozen sightings in a single month, then it may not be seen again for a year or more.

Witnesses have as much trouble describing Ogopogo as they have in describing Nessie. Some estimate its length at twenty feet (6.06 m); others say it is at least seventy feet (21.23 m) long. Some see flippers and some don't. Colors range from white to gray to black. It has been described as everything from snake-like to whalelike. One person will see tusks, and another won't even see teeth. A number of people see a short, rounded tail, and about an equal number see a forked tail.

There is probably an explanation for this. It seems that both Nessie and Ogopogo have been around for several hundred years. This, in turn, means that there has to be a number of Nessies and Ogopogos. A monster on its own could not survive for such a period of time. It would have to have a family. Naitaka, in fact, may have been Ogopogo's great-grandfather. Perhaps the monster found dead on the beach was a nephew of Naitaka's. A tadpole doesn't look like a frog, and perhaps a baby monster doesn't resemble a full-grown monster. We don't know that this is true, of course, but monsters have had people guessing for many, many years.

Since 1950 sightings of Ogopogo have become fairly common events. The exact number is not known, but several hundred people claim to have seen him. Lake Okanagan has grown into a very popular resort area. Visitors go there to ski, skate, hunt, fish, sail, and swim, and all of them keep an eye out for Ogopogo.

One group of tourists had particularly good luck. They were traveling along the shore of the lake in a Greyhound bus when a little old lady leaped to her feet. "There's Ogopogo!" she shrilled, pointing out the window. "There's the monster!"

And she was right. Ogopogo was not in a hurry that afternoon, and the tourists watched him slicing leisurely through the water. Although the road was quite high above the lake, they could all see a smallish head and a number of humps. Cameras clicked madly, but the distance was too great to get a decent photograph.

The next person to report a sighting that summer was the Reverend Walter S. Beames. Ministers never tell lies—not even about monsters—so the story has to be true.

It was late on a hot August afternoon that the Reverend Mr. Beames saw Ogopogo. There was no hint of a breeze, and the lake was perfectly calm. The minister was enjoying the peace and quiet when his thoughts were interrupted by a terrific commotion in the water. A series of humps rose above the surface. Neither the head nor the tail could be seen, but something was lashing around furiously. The commotion lasted only for a few seconds, then the creature swam off leaving a great wake. A hundred yards (91 m) from shore the truck-tire-size humps disappeared one by one into the depths.

Richard Miller is another man whose report has to be believed. He was the publisher of *The Vernon Advertiser* and had faithfully published many articles on Ogopogo. The account of his own meeting with the monster appeared in his column in the *Advertiser* on July 20, 1959.

One of the Miller children spotted the monster while the family was out cruising on the lake. Fortunately, the father had his field glasses with him and was able to get a very good look. Ogopogo was only about two hundred fifty feet (75.83 m) from them and traveling at nearly twice the speed of the boat. It was gliding gracefully through the water, but it was impossible to determine how it was pushing itself forward. It was not slithering sideways like a snake. There was no sign of flippers, fins, or tail. This doesn't mean, of course, that the creature doesn't have any or all of these things. It simply means that Miller didn't see them. He knew that Ogopogo had a tail, and he suspected that there might be fins or flippers between the humps.

The Miller family had the chance to watch the monster for three full minutes before it submerged. They all agreed that the five large humps were a very dark green. The head was definitely snakelike, and it had a blunt nose. They were unable to estimate the total length, however, because they had no way of knowing how much of the creature was beneath the surface. It was approximately twenty-five feet (7.58 m) from the nose to the fifth hump, they thought, and that was all they could say.

A monster of that size could frighten anyone, and on another occasion, it certainly gave poor fifteen-year-old Kenny Unser a bad scare. Kenny was playing with his dog near the old wharf in Kelowna. He would throw a stick into the lake, and the dog would jump off the end of the pier and fetch it. The game was good fun, but it came to an abrupt halt.

Young Unser was just getting ready to throw the stick when he noticed a strange disturbance in the water. Although the lake was calm, waves had suddenly begun to roll in toward the pier. Something peculiar was going on about seventy-five yards (68.58 m) from the shore, and he wondered what it could be.

While the boy stood watching, a head popped up in a shower

of spray. Things that looked like truck tires popped up behind it. Kenny had seen enough. He had been born in Kelowna, and he had heard about Ogopogo all his life. Meeting the monster face to face was the last thing he wanted to do. Without even taking a second look, the boy spun around and raced for home.

It's too bad that Kenny Unser didn't get a better description of the monster, but we can't really blame him. If Ogopogo suddenly popped up in front of one of us, we'd most likely do the same thing. We're lucky, in fact, that Kenny saw as much as he did. He said that the head was like a goat's and was dark green in color. The humps were larger than the head and were thick and heavy. If the thing had ears or horns, he said, he didn't see them. He was only interested in getting out of there as quickly as he could.

In the summer of 1970 a young lady from Vancouver came to Lake Okanagan for her annual three-weeks vacation. She enjoyed horseback riding and usually went out early in the morning. Her favorite ride was along the lake shore south of Kelowna.

The young lady had been riding for over an hour one morning. It was a particularly warm day, and she dismounted and sat down on a rock. The scenery was beautiful, and she sat looking out over the lake. The reins were held loosely in one hand.

The peaceful scene ended with fearful abruptness! The horse suddenly whinnied, reared straight up on its hind legs, then jerked the reins free and took off like a shot. The young lady immediately jumped to her feet—and it was then that she saw the creature! It was enormous and it was terrifying. It was also frighteningly close to shore. Like Kenny Unser, she had no interest at all in hanging around to get a good look. She took off at a run and didn't stop running until she reached her hotel.

"Well, what did the thing look like?" people in the hotel asked her when she'd told them her story.

"I don't know. I only saw it for half a second and even that was too long," she told them.

"But can't you describe it for us?" someone inquired.

"I just don't know. It—it—it looked like—something prehistoric. Like—like—" And then she thought she had the answer. "It looked just exactly like the Loch Ness Monster, I guess," she said.

Nobody, of course, knows just exactly what Nessie looks like, but everyone knew exactly what she meant. People have always found it difficult to describe monsters, and the young lady from Vancouver was no exception.

OTHER
LAKE M

ONSTERS

Monsters have supposedly been seen in quite a number of lakes in the United States and Canada. Reports of sightings have come in from Alaska, British Columbia, Manitoba, Quebec, Nevada, Montana, Idaho, Minnesota, Wisconsin, Oregon, California, and Vermont.

It wouldn't be wise to take all of these reports too seriously. The monster in Lake Walker, Nevada, for example, is supposed to be a man-eater. It made a special arrangement with the Indians in the last century, however, and since that time has eaten only white men.

A monster nicknamed Slimy Slim made the headlines in 1941, and there was even an article about it in *Time* magazine in August of that year.

Actually, Slimy Slim had reportedly been seen in Lake Payette, Idaho, long before 1941. Early settlers claimed to have seen something that vaguely resembled a huge crocodile. It was somewhere between thirty-five and fifty feet (9.70 and 15.16 m) long and had a head like a walrus. Nobody knows what happened to Slimy Slim, but he simply dropped out of the news. He was a celebrity one day and a has-been the next.

Wisconsin has thousands of lakes, and there have been monster reports from at least nine of them. The most convincing one comes from Lake Monona, which lies practically in the shadow of the state's capital in Madison. For a time the monster popped up every year, and the following article appeared in the *Wisconsin State Journal* on July 12, 1897.

Sea Serpent Appears Early This Year
What-Is-It in the Lake?

The Monona sea serpent has made its appearance about two months earlier than usual this season, according to several people in the vicinity of East Madison, who claim that they saw the monster last evening.

They say it was at least 30 feet [9.14 m] long and traveled east on the surface of the lake until Eugene Heath, agent of the Gaar-Scott Company, caused it to submerge by firing two shots into it. It is probably the same animal which is credited with having swallowed a dog which was swimming in the lake a few days ago. Mr. Schott and others who saw the "thing," whatever it may be, insist that it is a reality and not a joke or a creature of their combined imaginations.

Its appearance is not that of a serpent. Mr. Schott says that he saw it plainly and that its shape was like the bottom of a boat, but about twice as long. Mr. Schott's two sons saw it, and were so firmly convinced that it was a dangerous animal that when two ladies desired to be rowed over to Lakeside neither of the Schotts, who had spent a large part of their lives on the lake, would venture out.

A curious monster, perhaps the same sea serpent, was also observed off the Tonywatha and Winnequah shores, on the east side of the lake, by different persons.

It seems strange that the creature in Lake Monona was not investigated more thoroughly. While it's true that the University of Wisconsin was only a fledgling institution in 1897, there must have been a few scientists there who would have been interested enough to look into the matter. Lake Monona, after all, is less than a mile (1.61 km) from the university campus. Like so many men of science today, the scientists of 1897 probably thought that they would appear ridiculous if they went off monster hunting.

Fortunately, not all scientists are afraid of ridicule. One who certainly is not is Dr. James A. MacLeod, chairman of the Zoology Department of the University of Manitoba. He believes that primitive animals, long thought to be extinct, might still exist in some places. And he isn't afraid to say so!

Dr. MacLeod's favorite monster lives in Lake Manitoba, and its name is Manipogo. This is a take-off on the monster in Lake

Okanagan, of course, but Ogopogo probably has more important things than that to worry about.

Lake Manitoba covers an area of nearly two thousand square miles (5,180 sq. km). That's a lot of territory, so it's not surprising that Manipogo isn't sighted as often as Nessie or Ogopogo. In fact, it is frequently not seen for years at a time.

As has happened in other places, the monster figured strongly in the local Indian legends. The early settlers were told that there was a strange creature in the lake, and some of them claimed that they had seen it. Then, in 1909, a trader for the Hudson's Bay Company managed to get a fairly good look at the monster. It was swimming along very slowly, he said. The head was underwater, but about four feet (1.21 m) of its body was above the surface. The trader believed that the total length of the creature could not be less than thirty-five feet (10.61 m).

As far as is known, the monster was not seen again until twenty-six years later. Two timber inspectors, Charles Ross and Tom Spence, then told the *Winnipeg Free Press* that they had seen a most peculiar thing at the north end of the lake. It had a small, flat head, but the huge body was shaped like a dinosaur. The hide was a dull gray—about the same color as an elephant's and just as wrinkled.

This report caused some raised eyebrows. The Loch Ness Monster was big news in 1935, and the description given by the two timber inspectors was uncomfortably close to some of the descriptions given of Nessie. No one dared to say that they were telling a tall tale, but it seemed to be just too much of a coincidence.

Another twenty years went by before Manipogo once again made the front page of the local newspapers. In August 1955, Albert Gott, his two sons, and Joseph Parker saw an object rise about four feet (1.21 m) out of the water. It was a dark gray mass which they all thought looked oval-shaped, smooth, and slimy. It couldn't be an otter or a beaver or a seal, and it definitely wasn't a fish. The men didn't know what it was, but they knew that it was unlike anything they had ever seen before.

After the August 1955 sighting, Manipogo began popping up all over the place. It was reported so often that the Manitoba Department of Game and Fisheries decided to investigate. Government boats chugged back and forth across the lake for several weeks. Men with binoculars strained their eyes and saw nothing. Six other people, however, reported seeing the monster while the government team was out looking for it.

The summer of 1960 was a very busy time for Manipogo. Archie Adams of St. Rose saw it from the shore while he was casting for pike. It looked like a huge snake and appeared to be swimming at about fifteen miles (24 km) per hour. Adams was not able to see the body, but he guessed that it was much larger than the head and neck.

Mr. Christopher Stople, his wife, and his sister-in-law had a frightening experience the next day. They were fishing near Graves' Point when an "enormous reptilelike beast" surfaced only thirty feet (9.14 m) from their boat. The two women went wild with fear. Stople stared for a fraction of a second, then started the motor and raced for home. Nobody had ever before been that close to Manipogo, and it was much too close for comfort.

Unfortunately, the descriptions given by the three people are of little value. They were frightened out of their minds, and that is certainly understandable. The women could only say that the monster was huge, hideous, ugly, and things like that. Stople said it looked like something halfway between a snake and a dragon. He thought that it might have had teeth or tusks and that the color was either dark gray or light black. Stople readily admits, though, that he was much more interested in getting away from the monster than he was in studying it.

Twenty people, one of them a Canadian government official named Thomas Locke, watched Manipogo from Manipogo Beach on July 22. Three weeks later, on August 12, 1960, seventeen people saw *three* monsters from the same beach. Judging by the size, they were Papa Monster, Mama Monster, and Baby Monster.

The sudden flurry of sightings got Dr. James A. MacLeod all excited. Surely all of those people couldn't have seen something that didn't exist, he reasoned. There was definitely an unidentified creature of some kind in Lake Manitoba, and he was determined to find out what it was.

Unfortunately, the two expeditions led by Dr. MacLeod ended in failure. Luck was simply not on his side. The reports kept coming in, but he was never in the right place at the right time. On one occasion seven people watched Manipogo from Twin Beaches for nearly five minutes. Dr. MacLeod and a part of his team arrived less than an hour later. By that time, of course, the monster had taken off for parts unknown.

Two fishermen, Richard Vincent and John Konefell, and a Canadian television cameraman had much better luck. They managed to get the first photograph ever taken of the monster. It wasn't a terribly good photograph, but it did show an unidentified something in the lake.

"We first spotted the object to the left of our boat about three hundred yards (274.32 m) away," said Richard Vincent. "After swinging into the direction in which it was heading, we saw what we believed to be either a huge black snake or an eel. The back was at least a foot [.30 m] across and about twelve feet [3.66 m] of the monster was well above the water. At no time were we able to see the head or tail. We were about fifty to seventy-five yards [45.72 m to 68.58 m] away when the photograph was taken."

Dr. MacLeod studied the photograph at great length and stated his belief that it was genuine. "If this isn't a photo of the monster," he said to a reporter on the *Winnipeg Free Press*, "then I'd like to know just exactly what in the world it really is." Then he added, "In certain respects, it very closely resembles photographs taken of the monster in Loch Ness."

This doesn't necessarily mean that Manipogo and Nessie are related in any way. The photograph, however, may be one more bit of evidence proving that there actually are monsters in the fresh-water lakes of North America.

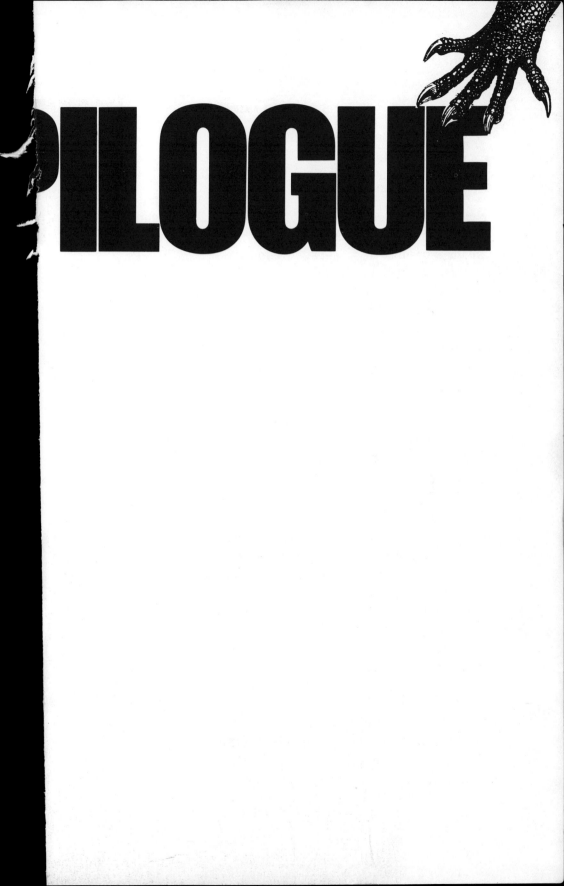

PILOGUE

Are there really monsters swimming and roaming around on the North American continent today? Do unidentified creatures still exist in our swamps, forests, mountains, lakes, and rivers? These are questions that we would all love to have answered for us.

Scientists are cautious men who normally demand proof. Many of them would not believe in the Fouke Monster, for example, even if it walked through their front door. They would think that their eyes were playing tricks on them. Unless the monster was captured or found dead, they would refuse to say that it existed. It would be awfully hard to convince Bobby Ford, however, that he was not attacked by a monster that terrifying night in Fouke, Arkansas. It would also be extremely difficult to convince Roger Patterson that he didn't get a photograph of Bigfoot near Bluff Creek, California, in 1967.

There have been hoaxes and false reports, of course, and probably a lot of them. Some people will go to any length to get their names in the paper. If a monster has been sighted anywhere in the area, they'll rush over to the nearest newspaper office and swear that they've seen it. On the other hand, some people report what they have seen but ask the papers not to use their names. John Green believes that many sightings are not even reported because the witnesses fear ridicule.

It may very well be the fear of ridicule which makes so many scientists reluctant to discuss monsters or admit they believe that they actually exist. Fortunately, there are some notable exceptions: Dr. Robert Rines of Boston has been chasing monsters for years. Zoologist Ivan Sanderson spent much of his time trying to track down unidentified animals. Dr. John Napier declared that he firmly believed in the existence of Bigfoot. Dr. James Mac-Leod risked ridicule by leading expeditions to Lake Manitoba to find Manipogo. Texan Tom R. Slick spent many thousands of dollars in his search for strange creatures in Lake Iliamna,

Alaska. None of these men solved any great mysteries of nature, but they at least had the courage to try.

Every zoologist must dream of making some discovery which will shake the scientific world. Fortunately, this is a dream that can still come true. Many questions have not yet been answered, and there are surprises in store for those who refuse to believe that some unusual creatures still exist on our earth. One zoologist who had a big surprise in store for him was Dr. J. L. Smith of Rhodes University in South Africa.

While in the Comoro Islands, Dr. Smith heard about a most peculiar fish which was sometimes caught in the fishermen's nets. The zoologist was intrigued. It sounded as though the fishermen were describing a coelacanth, but that hardly seemed possible. The coelacanth, he believed, had been extinct for about fifty million years. Nevertheless, he made arrangements to have the next specimen caught shipped to him in South Africa.

The islanders kept their word, and Dr. Smith received a large and rather smelly package in 1953. He opened it in his laboratory, and his eyes popped! A repulsive fish about five feet (1.51 m) long was lying on the bottom on a bed of dry grass. Soft, hollow spines ran up and down the length of its ugly, scaly body. Everything about the creature was hideous, but Dr. Smith thought that it was the most beautiful fish he had ever seen in his life.

When scientists heard about Smith's discovery, they gulped in astonishment. They all knew that the coelacanth belonged to the Triassic Age. It had been extinct for millions of years, so what right did it have to be swimming around in the Indian Ocean in the twentieth century? Fossils weren't supposed to behave that way. Once something became extinct, it was supposed to stay extinct.

The coelacanth, of course, had never been extinct at all. It had been swimming cheerfully around since ages past. The Comoran fishermen didn't know that it was a living fossil they occasionally caught in their nets. They simply looked upon it as a particularly ugly fish. It probably surprised them greatly to hear that the South African scientist wanted to have one sent to him.

Scientists are generally reluctant to say that something exists unless there is positive proof of its existence. This could be either a living creature or a dead one. If Dr. Smith had not had the dead body of a coelacanth, he could never have convinced the scientific world that such creatures were still around.

This is also true in the case of the unidentified monsters of North America. They have been seen by thousands of reputable people. Several have been photographed and plaster of Paris casts have been made of the tracks of others.

Sadly, though, this isn't good enough for many of the scientists. They won't admit that they believe in the existence of Bigfoot, Ogopogo, Momo, the Honey Island Swamp Monster, or any of the other monsters. What's more, they probably won't believe in them until one is brought into their laboratories. Only a body is accepted as proof. Photographs, casts, and sworn affidavits by respected citizens are not. The fact that the "extinct" coelacanth suddenly popped up after an absence of fifty million years doesn't seem to have swayed their thinking.

The doubts of the scientists don't really concern us. We can make up our own minds. Nature still holds many unsolved mysteries, and the mystery of monsters is perhaps the most intriguing of them all. It's fun to believe that there are unidentified monsters in North America today, and we wish all of them the very best of luck.

BIBLIOGRAPHY

Barber, Richard. *A Dictionary of Fabulous Beasts.* New York: Walker, 1972.

Borges, Jorge. *Book of Imaginary Beings.* New York: Dutton, 1969.

Brown, Charles. *Sea Serpents—Wisconsin Occurrences of These Weird Watery Monsters.* Madison: Wisconsin Folklore Society, 1942.

Clarke, Sallie Ann. *The Lake Worth Monster.* Fort Worth, Texas: Texas Printers, 1969.

Cohen, Daniel. *Modern Look at Monsters.* New York: Dodd, Mead, 1970.

Costello, Peter. *In Search of Lake Monsters.* St. Albans, Herts, England: Panther, 1975.

Cox, William. *Fearsome Creatures of the Lumberlands.* River Falls, Wisconsin: State University Press, 1910.

Deane, Ernie. *Ozarks Country.* Republic, Missouri: Western Printing, 1975.

Dinsdale, Tim. *The Leviathans.* London: Routledge and Kegan Paul, 1966.

Edwards, Frank. *Stranger Than Science.* New York: Bantam, 1967.

Gould, Charles. *Mythical Monsters.* London: W. H. Allen, 1886.

Green, John. *The Sasquatch File.* Agassiz, British Columbia: Cheam Publishing, 1973.

Heuvelmans, Bernard. *On the Track of Unknown Animals*. London: Rupert Hart-Davis, 1958.

Heuvelmans, Bernard. *In the Wake of the Sea-Serpents*. London: Rupert Hart-Davis, 1968.

Laycock, George. *Strange Monsters and Great Searches*. New York: Doubleday, 1973.

Ley, Willie. *The Lungfish, the Dodo and the Unicorn*. New York: Viking, 1949.

Lum, Peter. *Fabulous Beasts*. New York: Pantheon, 1951.

Marchant, R. A. *Beasts of Fact and Fable*. New York: Roy Publishers, 1962.

McHargue, Georgess. *Beasts of Never*. New York: Bobbs-Merrill, 1968.

Miller, Carey. *A Dictionary of Monsters and Mysterious Beasts*. London: Pan, 1974.

Roosevelt, Theodore. *Wilderness Hunter*. New York: G. P. Putnam's Sons, 1893.

Slate, Ann, and Berry, Alan. *Bigfoot*. Bantam, 1976.

Soule, Gardner. *Maybe Monsters*. New York: G. P. Putnam's Sons, 1963.

Spence, Lewis. *The Myths of the North American Indians*. New York: Farrar and Rinehart, 1932.

Stuart, Dorothy. *A Book of Birds and Beasts*. London: Methuen, 1957.

Thompson, C. J. *Mystery and Lore of Monsters*. Secaucus, New Jersey: Citadel, 1970.

White, T. H. *The Book of Beasts*. London: Jonathan Cape, 1954.

Wyman, Walker. *Mythical Creatures of the North Country*. River Falls, Wisconsin: State University Press, 1969.

INDEX

ABOUT THE AUTHOR

While researching *The Loch Ness Monster* and *Bigfoot* for Franklin Watts, Elwood Baumann kept hearing and reading about other monsters in the American lakes, swamps, forests, and mountains. Fascinated by these lesser-known monsters, he decided that a book on the subject would also interest young readers.

Elwood D. Baumann was born in Saskatchewan, Canada, and is a graduate of the University of Wisconsin. After many years as a teacher and principal in schools in Turkey and Venezuela, he took up writing as a vocation and travel as an avocation. He has now traveled in 105 countries on 6 continents.

Mr. Baumann has lived in the Scottish Highlands and has written about the Loch Ness Monster. He is an enthusiastic member of the North American Wildlife Research Association and firmly believes in Bigfoot. His fascinating accounts of both of these strange creatures are published by Franklin Watts. Mr. Baumann is also the author of three other Franklin Watts titles: *They Came From Space, The Devil's Triangle,* and *Vampires.*